FROM EL GRECO
TO POLLOCK:

EARLY
AND
LATE
WORKS

BY EUROPEAN AND
AMERICAN ARTISTS

EDITED BY
GERTRUDE ROSENTHAL

A PUBLICATION OF
THE BALTIMORE MUSEUM OF ART
Distributed by
New York Graphic Society Ltd.
Greenwich, Connecticut

FROM EL GRECO TO POLLOCK:
EARLY AND LATE WORKS
BY EUROPEAN AND AMERICAN ARTISTS
Dates of the exhibition:
October 22 through December 8, 1968

Copyright© 1968 The Baltimore Museum of Art
Wyman Park, Baltimore, Maryland 21218
Printed in the United States of America
Library of Congress Catalogue Card No. 68-58201
SBN 8212-1207-9

CONTENTS

FOREWORD   7
    Charles Parkhurst

ACKNOWLEDGEMENTS   8

LENDERS TO THE EXHIBITION   9

INTRODUCTION   11
    Gertrude Rosenthal

CATALOGUE OF THE EXHIBITION   15
AND COMMENTS

SELECTED BIBLIOGRAPHY   168

INDEX OF ARTISTS   178

FOREWORD

This catalogue is a permanent record of a fascinating undertaking, an exhibition which was first envisioned, then designed and coordinated by Dr. Gertrude Rosenthal. Although it is my principal duty here to express our deepest thanks to the lenders who made the exhibition of Early and Late Works possible, I am moved to dwell for a moment on a comment by Professor Richard A. Macksey: "In contemporary American Society the accent, as the advertisements say, is on youth. . . . The familiar image of the poet in such a society is too often that of a precocious artist burned out on the ledge of a fiery adolescence, discreetly dying in his early majority."

The present exhibition gives the lie to any romantic notion that such was the case with many of our great artists of the past and present. The "sea changes" in the life style of most of these artists, represented over a substantial span of years by pairs of pictures in this exhibition, suggest that the romantic notion does *not* apply and that no formula can be used to explain or to predict what the old age product of an artist will become. Although it seems likely that essential tendencies of mind are already established in young artists, commitment to these ideas, viewed with insight and outwardly revealed through increasing facility of the hand, often produce in a great artist's later years absolute and stunning manifestations born of his commitment, dexterity and thought.

The revelation of an artist's spiritual and mental course depends, of course, on the quality of these manifestations, for quality is an exponent of revelation in art. This is abundantly expressed in the present exhibition and for this we have the lenders to thank.

I wish to acknowledge our appreciation to them all — twenty-five private lenders and sixty museums, for their great courtesy in supporting this exhibition so willingly. Their loans reflect, in quality and importance, signal generosity on their part; but I also construe their response as a recognition of our great Chief Curator on the eve of her retirement for, *tempus abire* — this is her last official show before she leaves us for a while to pursue her own research, a somewhat chilling moment which will be tempered for her by the warmth of this personal and professional support.

Although Dr. Rosenthal has thanked the contributors of the comparative essays to this catalogue, from whose efforts you can only get pleasure and instruction, I want to add my personal appreciation. Their writing has made this book, like the exhibition upon which it is based, a significant addition to earlier studies of this theme.

Charles Parkhurst
Director

ACKNOWLEDGEMENTS

For the comments in this catalogue we are indebted to the following authors:

Adelyn D. Breeskin, *Special Consultant and Curator of Contemporary Art,* National Collection of Fine Arts, Smithsonian Institution, Washington, D. C.; *Director Emeritus,* The Baltimore Museum of Art

Grose Evans, *Curator,* Index of American Design, National Gallery of Art, Washington, D. C.

Henry Geldzahler, *Curator of Contemporary Arts,* The Metropolitan Museum of Art, New York

Lloyd Goodrich, *Advisory Director,* Whitney Museum of American Art, New York

Donald E. Gordon, *Professor,* Department of Fine Art, Dickinson College, Carlisle, Pennsylvania

Lawrence Gowing, *Professor,* Department of Fine Arts, The University of Leeds, England

Christopher Gray, *Associate Professor,* Department of History of Art, The Johns Hopkins University, Baltimore

Diana F. Johnson, *Assistant Curator of Painting and Sculpture,* The Baltimore Museum of Art

Lincoln Johnson, *Professor,* Department of Fine Arts, Goucher College, Towson, Maryland

Marian Willard Johnson, *Director,* Willard Gallery, Inc., New York

Edward S. King, *Research Associate,* Walters Art Gallery, Baltimore

Hilton Kramer, *Critic, The New York Sunday Times,* New York

Alain de Leiris, *Associate Professor,* Department of Art, University of Maryland, College Park

Abram Lerner, *Curator,* Joseph H. Hirshhorn Collection, New York

George Levitine, *Professor,* Department of Art, University of Maryland, College Park

John A. Mahey, *Assistant Director,* The Peale Museum, Baltimore

Howard S. Merritt, *Professor,* Department of Fine Arts, The University of Rochester, New York

Thomas M. Messer, *Director,* The Solomon R. Guggenheim Museum, New York

Michael Milkovich, *Director,* University Art Gallery, State University of New York, Binghamton

Francis V. O'Connor, *Assistant Professor,* Department of Art, University of Maryland, College Park

Roger Rearick, *Assistant Professor,* Department of History of Art, The Johns Hopkins University, Baltimore

Edgar P. Richardson, *Former Director,* The Henry Francis du Pont Winterthur Museum, Delaware

John Richardson, *Author and critic,* also U. S. Representative, Christie, Manson & Woods, Ltd., New York

Daniel Robbins, *Director,* Museum of Art, Rhode Island School of Design, Providence

Eric Van Schaack, *Assistant Professor,* Department of Fine Arts, Goucher College, Towson, Maryland

Peter Selz, *Director,* University Art Museum, University of California, Berkeley

Seymour Slive, *Professor,* Department of Fine Arts, Harvard University, Cambridge, Massachusetts

Allen Staley, *Assistant Curator of Paintings,* Philadelphia Museum of Art

Wolfgang Stechow, *Professor Emeritus,* History of Art, Oberlin College, Ohio; *Advisory Curator of European Art,* Cleveland Museum of Art

Frank Andersen Trapp, *Professor,* Department of Art History, Amherst College, Massachusetts

Ellis Waterhouse, *Director,* Barber Institute of Fine Arts, University of Birmingham, England

Ila Weiss, *Researcher* in American nineteenth-century art

Robert P. Welsh, *Assistant Professor,* Department of Fine Art, University of Toronto

John White, *Professor,* Department of History of Art, The Johns Hopkins University, Baltimore

Mahonri Sharp Young, *Director,* The Columbus Gallery of Fine Arts, Ohio

LENDERS TO THE EXHIBITION

Colonel Samuel A. Berger, New York; Mr. and Mrs. Jacob Blaustein, Baltimore; Clowes Fund Collection, Indianapolis; Mrs. Abram Eisenberg, Baltimore; Mr. and Mrs. Allan Frumkin, New York; Mr. and Mrs. Victor W. Ganz, New York; Mrs. Edith Gregor Halpert, New York; Joseph H. Hirshhorn Collection and Foundation, New York; Mrs. Samuel E. Johnson, Chicago; Mr. and Mrs. David Lloyd Kreeger, Washington, D.C.; Mr. and Mrs. Robert E. Meyerhoff, Baltimore; Mr. and Mrs. I. David Orr, New York; Mrs. Lee Krasner Pollock, New York; Mr. and Mrs. Gustave Ring, Washington, D.C.; Dr. and Mrs. Israel Rosen, Baltimore; Mr. Charles Coleman Sellers, Carlisle, Pennsylvania; Mrs. Albert Sperry, Los Angeles; Mr. and Mrs. Charles Zadok, New York.

Albright-Knox Art Gallery, Buffalo, New York; Allen Memorial Art Museum, Oberlin College, Ohio; Art Gallery of Ontario, Toronto; The Art Institute of Chicago; Bowdoin College Museum of Art, Brunswick, Maine; Brandeis University Art Collection, Waltham, Massachusetts; The Brooklyn Museum, New York; The Butler Institute of American Art, Youngstown, Ohio; California Palace of the Legion of Honor, San Francisco; Cincinnati Art Museum; City Art Museum of St. Louis, Missouri; Sterling and Francine Clark Art Institute, Williamstown, Massachusetts; The Cleveland Museum of Art; Columbia Museum of Art, South Carolina; Columbus Gallery of Fine Arts, Ohio; The Corcoran Gallery of Art, Washington, D.C.; Cummer Gallery of Art, Jacksonville, Florida; Dallas Museum of Fine Arts, Texas; Dayton Art Institute, Ohio; The Detroit Institute of Arts; Fogg Art Museum, Harvard University, Cambridge, Massachusetts; The Solomon R. Guggenheim Museum, New York; Herron Museum of Art Indianapolis; John G. Johnson Collection, Philadelphia; The Los Angeles County Museum of Art; Lyman Allyn Museum, New London, Connecticut; Marion Koogler McNay Art Institute, San Antonio, Texas; The Maryland Institute College of Art, Baltimore; The Metropolitan Museum of Art, New York; The Montclair Art Museum, New Jersey; Munson-Williams-Proctor Institute, Utica, New York; Museum of Art, Carnegie Institute, Pittsburgh; Museum of Fine Arts, Boston; The Museum of Fine Arts, Houston, Texas; Museum of Fine Arts, Springfield, Massachusetts; The Museum of Modern Art, New York; National Gallery of Art, Washington, D.C.; The National Gallery of Canada, Ottawa; Nelson Gallery-Atkins Museum, Kansas City, Missouri; New York State Historical Association, Cooperstown; North Carolina Museum of Art, Raleigh; The Peabody Institute, Baltimore; The Pennsylvania Academy of the Fine Arts, Philadelphia; Philadelphia Museum of Art; The Phillips Collection, Washington, D.C.; Portland Art Museum, Oregon; John and Mable Ringling Museum of Art, Sarasota, Florida; Santa Barbara Museum of Art, California; Smith College Museum of Art, Northampton, Massachusetts; Stedelijk Museum, Vincent van Gogh Foundation, Amsterdam; The Taft Museum, Cincinnati; The Tate Gallery, London; University Art Museum, University of California, Berkeley; The University of Arizona Art Gallery, Tucson; University of Nebraska, Lincoln; Victoria and Albert Museum, London; Wadsworth Atheneum, Hartford, Connecticut; The Walters Art Gallery, Baltimore; Washington University, St. Louis, Missouri; Worcester Art Museum, Massachusetts; M. H. De Young Memorial Museum, San Francisco.

Allan Frumkin Gallery, New York; Marlborough-Gerson Gallery, Inc., New York; Perls Galleries, New York; Wildenstein and Co., Inc., New York; Willard Gallery, New York.

The exhibition "From El Greco to Pollock: Early and Late Works by European and American Artists," as well as this publication accompanying it, is focused on two major phases in the development of seventy painters chosen from four centuries. It deals with the phenomena of change and continuity which in the light of today's young generation's new assessment of values are wrought with special meaning. In the context of our subject these phenomena are examined only in a very limited area — that of artistic expression in the styles of masters of the past and our time. Juxtaposing a representative example of each artist's early and late works, we have pondered the question of how consistent his style — his "handwriting" — has remained from the beginning to the termination of his career. We have further wondered whether, and if so to what extent, the continuity of concept (as evident, for example, in Matisse's oeuvre) affects the transformations and changes of style. Does it rule them out or can it co-exist with them? And then there is that most vexing problem, which perhaps is unanswerable: can a definite pattern be recognized in the creative personality's artistic development that is in any way comparable to the pattern of biological maturation which exists despite differences between every individual.

While practically every artist's biography mentions the subject's early manner in reference to his later output, few studies have been devoted to a more generic exploration of these two poles in the creative process and their relation to each other. The first concentrated treatise of the theme was A. E. Brinckmann's *Spätwerke Grosser Meister* (Late Works by Great Masters) which, published in 1925, was widely read and has become a kind of classic. Attempting to define the specific qualities of "the late style" which he equates with works produced by artists over sixty, Brinckmann promulgates the theory that these creations share certain features, among which the fusion or the blending (*Verschmelzung*) of all compositional elements is the most characteristic. Elaborating on this idea, he names as attributes of the late style a decrease of dynamic movement, an even tonality, muted color, disinterest in detail, a lessening of tension and the attainment of not only pictorial unity but also harmony in expression. Brinckmann's findings are still provocative, but in this writer's opinion they are valid in their entirety only if applied to a small select group consisting mainly of the masters he has used as examples for his thesis.

Exactly forty years after the publication of Brinckmann's book, another well-known German art historian, Joseph Gantner, has treated the same subject in an essay "The Old Artist" (1965, pp. 71-76). Although Gantner follows Brinckmann in accepting the existence of a definite "old-age style," he realizes the variety and diversity of its manifestations and thus conveys the complexity of the problem. Much broader in his concepts which therefore are more applicable than Brinckmann's common denominator of the late manner, Gantner recognizes as a general criterion the old artist's disregard for clearly articulated form and finished appearance which in late works are often replaced by a freer, a more sketch-like quality.

Relating Gantner's remarkably undogmatic and loose definition to the contents of our exhibition, we discover that it describes certain aspects of the late works of major artists from various periods. In addition to Rembrandt, Hals and Rubens — classic examples of old-age style — Gantner's formulation fits the late paintings of Poussin, Goya, Guardi, Tiepolo, Gainsborough, Delacroix, Monet, Pissarro, Cézanne, Braque and Corinth; to these might be added Turner despite, in Lawrence Gowing's words, "the strangely violent tissue of the last pictures" and Picasso, who as an octogenarian has begun to pay less attention to structure and has produced the most painterly works of his long career. But what about El Greco, Claude Lorrain, Copley, Ingres, Eakins, Kandinsky, Léger, Marin, Mondrian or Matisse and many others who either have continued with minor transformations the paths they had entered in the years of their youth or maturity or have found new solutions as for example did Mondrian and Matisse — solutions that do not reveal any of the characteristics associated with the old-age style as outlined above.

Another attempt at determining the specific properties of early and late works should also be mentioned, especially since it was made — though on a comparatively small scale — by this museum in 1954, when in a section of the exhibition "Man and His Years" we asked questions quite similar to those we have posed in the present exhibition. This time we have offered a much larger number of what we consider valid comparisons and have received the help of over thirty experts in defining the relations between the early and the late example of an individual artist's oeuvre. Guided by our authors' comments and also by scrutinizing once more the exhibition material, we no longer reject — as we did in our previous venture — the possible existence of certain related tendencies that may be detected in the late works of great masters who retained their creativity in old age. Of course this concession in no way denies the incomprehensible variety of individual responses of eminent painters.

We can agree with Walter Friedlaender's interpretation (1952, p. 131) of the old-age style as being "characterized by a deepening, a condensation, an increasing harmony of the underlying artistic concept. . . ." Although already inherent in this statement, we want to emphasize in this context the increase of intensity, whether it appears as internalization as it does in Rembrandt and Goya or as bursts of a new, last vitality as in El Greco, Turner and Matisse. The renunciation of virtuosity may also be cited as typical of the late creations of great artists who in their old age reached an assurance that made any display of showmanship superfluous. At this stage of their career these men did not hesitate to assert themselves: to quote the old Cézanne who felt that "there is only one painter alive today, myself," but who also said with profound modesty: "I am working stubbornly, I begin to see the promised land." It is an attitude not unusual for an old artist of any period. When in his eighties, Hans Hofmann, showing similar pride and similar humility, told this writer half-mockingly: "I have a great future ahead; remember that Titian did his best works after he was ninety years old." Becoming serious, he added: "I finally have gotten all the technical skill to say what I want. By now it's really up to me to paint the best pictures of my career. How I hope that I'll be able to. . . ."

In an inquiry into the characteristics of late styles, it is essential to differentiate between works created by masters in their old age and those by artists who died before their time. As long as the painters had clearly developed the two stylistic phases with which our project is concerned, the length of their life span had no bearing on their inclusion in this exhibition. When at last we considered the years of their artistic activities, we were amazed to find that a small number, approximately ten percent of those represented, had died before reaching fifty. Among them were van Dyck, van Gogh, Toulouse-Lautrec, Gorky and Pollock. Because the tragedy of the genius' early death seems unacceptable, the idea has been propagated that in many such instances the artist's maturation was accelerated so that his talent reached fulfillment — a myth which, though supported not only by romantic laymen but also by some psychologists, must be refuted (Gantner, 1965, p. 72). Yet the subject invites speculation: van Dyck's last words, in which elegance of content and technical bravura are the most conspicuous features, certainly cannot be considered anticipations of a late style. On the other hand, van Gogh's Auvers paintings, done during the last few months of his life, convey — at least to this writer — the whole gamut of serenity and tragic fate associated with the final accomplishments of an old master. In this connection we cannot help but think of Pollock, as endangered as he was endowed; if he had lived, could he have resolved the dichotomy between self and art and come to a full realization of his artistic concepts?

Excepting the exhibition and symposium "Youthful Works of Great Artists" (held in 1963 at Oberlin College) in which no general conclusions were sought, we do not know of any specific studies focused on a general evaluation of artists' early styles. No wonder: there seem to be few problems in art history that pose more difficulties and negate any general solutions. How to define the early phase in an artist's evolution? To this question there is no factual answer. Eliminating student works from our considerations, we searched for early manifestations of each artist's personal style. The paintings chosen according to our criterion of "early" do not necessarily date from the artist's period of physical youth. A few examples will suffice to indicate the difference in the ages of painters at the time they executed the works shown here as "early:" van Dyck was eighteen; Rembrandt twenty-six; Rubens thirty-one; Copley twenty; Degas, Sargent, Whistler and Vuillard were in their early twenties; Gauguin was thirty-six; Picasso twenty-one; Matisse, Mondrian and Kandinsky were close to forty; Dubuffet and Tobey were forty-five, and Hans Hofmann was sixty-three.

Aside from the availability of desirable pictures and the aesthetic merit of the individual object, our choices were mainly determined by the consideration of the artist's sustained creativity. Also the question whether an artist's beginning and ending phases were at all indicative of the extent of his contributions to art was carefully weighed and resulted in the omission of a number of great painters, among them Courbet.

The evaluation of a late style requires that each artist's career is considered in its entirety; our excuse for representing in this exhibition five living artists is based on our assumption that these men have reached the height of their achievements from which we could draw. In order to make the confrontation of each early and late work meaningful, we have searched for such examples in each artist's oeuvre that are not only typical and of high artistic quality but also facilitate comparison between the companion pieces. In two instances we have overruled our self-imposed limit of "two pictures per artist." We simply could not resist the temptation of providing four aspects of Picasso's multifaceted style; in the case of Matisse, we felt that, in addition to the two magnificent oils, the existence of his tremendously influential, last invention — his *gouaches découpées* — had to be acknowledged.

We are aware of our subjective approach to our theme and the ambivalence in some of our responses. Nevertheless, we hope that the questions we have posed will stimulate our visitors and readers to ponder the mysterious process of artistic creativity, as they study and compare the early and late works by great artists presented in this exhibition.

Despite long familiarity with certain aspects of our subject, the organization of this project has been a challenging and exciting experience. For having given us the opportunity to carry out this task, we are deeply indebted to Charles Parkhurst, Director, who eliminated many of the restrictions normally imposed by budget and schedule considerations, and who also counseled and supported us whenever necessary.

Our venture has involved hundreds of people, first of all the lenders who have made the realization of our project possible. We cannot adequately express our gratitude to the many experts who responded so nobly to our call for help by contributing to this book their comments on the early and late styles of the artists represented in the exhibition. Among our colleagues at the Baltimore Museum our special thanks are due to Diana F. Johnson who worked closely with me on this catalogue functioning as associate editor. We want to express our gratitude to Mary C. Dickerman who as special assistant took on many difficult duties pertaining to the exhibition and catalogue. It was a pleasure to work with Ann Allston Boyce, Supervisor of Publications, who carried her full load of responsibility, efficiently and enthusiastically. We further acknowledge the advice and help received from Susan Hamilton, Chief of Program, in all matters concerning the printing of this publication. Rima Parkhurst, inexpendable volunteer and an experienced editor, read the text in manuscript and made many useful suggestions. The museum's librarian, Anne Venables, helped with the preparation of the bibliography. Margaret M. Powell, Head of Installation, aided by the other members of her department, has tried to overcome the many installation problems posed by the theme of the exhibition and has succeeded in presenting the works of art to their full advantage. It is impossible to thank individually all our co-workers who have been involved in this major undertaking, but they must know how much their cooperation, extended beyond the call of duty, is appreciated.

Gertrude Rosenthal
Chief Curator

CATALOGUE
OF THE EXHIBITION
AND COMMENTS

References within the text are indicated in parentheses by a key name, date of publication and pertinent page. To get the full bibliographical information, readers should turn to the Selected Bibliography where each work is cited in full.

El Greco (Doménikos Theotokópoulos)
Greek (Spanish School), 1541-1614

That Doménikos Theotokópoulos rose above the ranks of the resident colony of mediocre Greek icon painters in Venice is in itself remarkable. That he achieved a measure of celebrity in competition with the xenophobic painters of the Roman establishment is evidence of his independent and aggressive spirit. On his arrival in Venice he sought out the most prestigious of studios, that of the aged Titian, in which to take his apprenticeship. Titian had a reputation for exploiting his pupils, working them hard and teaching them little, and it is unlikely that the young Cretan suffered this use lightly or long. Instead, he scavenged a magpie education by close observation of the Renaissance all around him. Tintoretto, Bassano, graphic arts of the North and of the circle of Michelangelo were his academy. The Venetians presided over huge family workshops which functioned smoothly for mass production; the immigrant Greek had no such establishment and decided to try his luck in the more individualistic atmosphere of Rome. There he is reported to have brazenly suggested that Michelangelo's colossal but controversial *Last Judgment* be torn from the wall of the Sistine Chapel and be replaced with his own treatment, which he ventured would be finer and more appropriate, even though he had probably never painted a fresco before. His arrogance cannot hide his fascination with the most revered of renaissance masters, an interest to which the early *Pietà* is an eloquent testament.

The composition of the *Pietà* depends less on Michelangelo's celebrated marble sculpture, now in the Florence cathedral, than on the mannered and rhetorical variants of that model then in vogue among his Roman followers. Doménikos makes of it a startlingly personal image. Using an encaustic-like medium of a strange transparency more closely related to his Greek origins than to the dense impasto of the Venetian school, he creates an aura of dematerialized fluidity in which interlocking forms merge landscape, sky and figures in an ambivalent spatial order. In place of the heroic expression of his models the young painter infuses the group with an intimate pathos. Iconic in its lonely simplicity, the scene is devoid of descriptive detail and suggestive, as in the robe of St. John at left, of a highly individual sense for abstracted form. It is hardly surprising that this odd style won only a few admirers in Rome. By 1576 it was clear that Doménikos would not be given any major commissions in Italy; in the spring of the following year he arrived in Toledo where he would remain until his death in 1614.

El Greco, as he was henceforth called, found the austere Counter Reformation religiosity of Spain a fertile inspiration to his feverish pictorial imagination. Always emotionally volatile and inclined to expressive distortion, he evolved a unique visionary style during the remaining thirty-seven years of his career. *St. Francis Kneeling in Meditation,* painted close to 1600, foreshadows his latest works in which rubbery shapes are transfixed by flashes of a cold lunar glare. Feather-soft brush strokes in the dove gray robe intensify into an incandescent flicker in the palely ascetic face, while the restless still life and the poison green leaves are charged with the same ecstatic inner life. Contrary to popular belief, neither dementia nor astigmatism contribute to this late style, but it is rather a keen intelligence, a fine-honed sensibility and an obedient brush which are at the service of his spirit.

Roger Rearick

1 PIETA c.1570-72
Tempera on panel; 11 1/8 x 8 inches
Signed in Greek capitals, lower left:
DOMENIKOS THEOTOKOPOULOS [E'POIEI?]
Lent from the John G. Johnson Collection

2   ST. FRANCIS
KNEELING IN MEDITATION   1595-1600
Oil on canvas; 58 x 41 1/2 inches
Signed in cursive Greek letters, lower right:
domenikos theotokopoulos e'poiei
Lent by the M. H. De Young Memorial Museum
Gift of Samuel H. Kress Foundation

Seventeenth
Century

Claude Lorrain (Claude Gellée)
French, 1600-82

Claude's artistic development is superficially as calm as the idyllic landscapes that he paints. There are no sweeping changes in content. There is no dramatic broadening of the brush stroke with old age. No sudden changes of direction make us wonder how the youth became the man. Like his individual paintings, his career responds to meditation, to the quiet unhurried contemplation that at first brings peace, and later, understanding. Beneath the placid surface of his art the movement is both deep and rich.

Claude's earliest surviving works date from the late 1620's and early 1630's. *The Flight into Egypt* is typical of the work which he was doing when his feet were firmly set upon the road he was to travel all his life. The relatively small scale, the biblical subject matter, the gentle pastoral lyricism, the delight in leaf and branch and tree, in plants and cattle, waterfalls and rocks, are to be found in many of his early works. The clear recession, plane by plane, without undue insistence upon measured space is also typical of his personal vision. Even in his early seaport scenes, in which he comes the closest to his great contemporary Nicolas Poussin, light from the setting sun invariably dissolves the stable architectural mathematics. This particular landscape is, indeed, amongst the most intimate of his productions, since the background does not open out into sunlit infinities of sea or over haze-lost, distant valleys to far mountains. Light dancing over form, revealing and dissolving the appearances of nature; light flickering on leaves, softening the detail, bathing it in a warm unifying glow that makes the trees the mediators between earth and air; this is the hallmark of the early work of Claude.

The landscape of *Parnassus with Minerva Visiting the Muses* is no less typical of Claude's last five years before his death in 1682. From the 1640's onwards classical themes are often interspersed with those drawn from the Bible, and in his final years they take on fresh importance as Ovid, the source for this particular scene, is joined by Vergil in Claude's reading. Instead of moving to a final thunder, the gravity and grandeur increasingly apparent in Claude's paintings of the sixties and seventies find their resolution in an ultimate calm. Here in the *Parnassus with Minerva* . . . is no dancing sun, but cool, clear light. There is grandeur of scale and composition and a classical subject treated with a classical serenity. The bold asymmetry of the design, replacing earlier tendencies to a more even balance, is a reminder that serenity is not softness. It is instead a distillation, in artistic terms, of wisdom and control.

Now the embattled mortal world has been left far below by the armed goddess. The onlooker stands in the company of the immortals in a grove on high Parnassus. The superhuman elongation of the figures in this, perhaps the finest of all of Claude's latest figure groups, creates the stature of a myth without accompanying earthbound bulk. In color, in security of mood and composition, and in delicacy of detail, these gravely welcoming figures are a final reminder that this is, indeed, a world of the ideal, more real than the reality which, like the distant landscape, slips away into the valleys of the mind.

It is only one of many historical illustrations of the power of art, of idylls and ideals, in the hands of great poets and great painters, that eighteenth-century Englishmen should not only have viewed the world through the tinted lenses of what were known as "Claude glasses," which made a varnished painting of reality, but also that they should have built their houses, planned the vistas in their parks, dug lakes, laboriously cast up hills and planted groves and spinneys, seeking to transform the English landscape in the image of the Claudes they carried home from the Grand Tour to hang upon their walls. Significantly, just as it was the unprecedented closeness of Claude's observation of the fundamentals of nature which gave his idyllic landscapes their compelling power, so the attempted imposition of this ideal upon the real world impelled a new understanding of nature.

Though its darker greens have sunk with time, and though the vision in certain details is now not quite as fresh as when it left Claude's hand and was drawn in the *Liber Veritatis*, his own record of his lifetime's work, the *Parnassus with Minerva* . . . serves as a summary of the more than fifty years during which Claude, with single-minded concentration and unfailing freshness of vision, lived within the liberating confines of a great tradition. Few painters have done more than Claude to enrich the life and in the process to transform the impact of an ideal which, in the western world, has delighted, formed, inspired, and haunted men's minds for so many centuries. The secret of his power lies in such paintings.

John White

3   THE FLIGHT INTO EGYPT   c.1635
Oil on canvas; 29 x 38 1/2 inches
Signed on stone, lower center: *CLAV IN* [illegible]
Lent from the Clowes Fund Collection

4   PARNASSUS WITH MINERVA
VISITING THE MUSES   1680
Oil on canvas; 57 x 76 inches
Signed, inscribed and dated lower right:
CLAUDIO IV ROMA 1680
Lent by the Cummer Gallery of Art

Anthony van Dyck
Flemish, 1599-1641

5 PORTRAIT OF A BEARDED MAN   1615-16
Oil on panel; 29 x 24 1/4 inches
Lent by the Allen Memorial Art Museum
Oberlin College

The term "artistic prodigy" is applicable to very few artists, but in the case of Anthony van Dyck it is unquestionably justified. By the time he was ten or eleven, he was already a pupil of Hendrick van Balen, head of the local artists' guild. At nineteen he was a Master in the guild and had a studio of his own. For several years he was associated with Rubens, who entrusted the highly gifted and ambitious van Dyck with the execution of several important commissions.

Van Dyck's *Portrait of a Bearded Man* is undocumented, but Wolfgang Stechow (1944, p. 299) has dated it 1615-16, placing it at the very beginning of van Dyck's artistic career. The loose brush strokes and freedom of handling are striking, and there is a liveliness and intimacy that set it apart from the general run of early seventeenth-century Flemish portraits with their carefully smoothed and finished surfaces. Although the man's identity is not known, the sense of individual character and a particular personality so pervades the portrait that one can hardly help speculating on the nature of the sitter. Benedict Nicolson has felt that the "evil, licentious eyes and mouth are unforgettable," (1962, p. 310) while Stechow has seen "an unmistakable touch of wistfulness." But whatever opinion we may form of the man's character, van Dyck's fresh and

6 PORTRAIT OF MARY,
DUCHESS OF LENNOX   1638-40
Oil on canvas; 83 x 40 inches
Lent by the North Carolina Museum of Art
Gift of Mrs. Theodore Webb

vigorous study is a truly remarkable performance.

More than twenty years later, van Dyck executed the *Portrait of Mary, Duchess of Lennox*, and the intervening years had seen the fulfillment of the brilliant promise of his early career. After a brief stay in England in 1620-21, he had gone to Italy, following in the footsteps of Rubens, and had established himself as the finest portrait painter of the day. In the late 1620's he returned to Antwerp where he remained until 1632 when he went to England once again. In England van Dyck was employed by Charles I as "principal painter in ordinary to their Majesties." In recognition of his services he was knighted and shown many signs of favor by the King, who often visited his studio. The royal portraits were a great success, and the English nobility was quick to follow the lead of their monarch.

Mary, daughter of George Villiers, first duke of Buckingham, had been married to Charles, Lord Herbert, before becoming in 1637 the wife of James Stuart, fourth duke of Lennox and first duke of Richmond. Both she and her second husband were often painted by van Dyck. Her portrait included in this exhibition is a fine example of the type of aristocratic portraiture that van Dyck introduced into England. The formal setting enhances the elegance and grace of her pose, so carefully contrived, yet seemingly so spontaneous. Her composure is undisturbed by the presence of the young child, personified as Cupid with the arrow of Love. Van Dyck's sensitivity to the personalities of his sitters and his keen grasp of their self-assurance led him to develop the pictorial formulae of the aristocratic portrait. This insight into character was matched by his brilliant technique. There is a softness, a delicacy which gives an almost dream-like quality to the portrait. He has completely abandoned the heavy pigment and bold spontaneity which characterized the *Portrait of a Bearded Man* in favor of a more finished effect; there is a silvery tonality, an emphasis on a variety of textures and a delight in subtle nuances of light and shade.

Van Dyck's English portraits revolutionized the art of portraiture in England and made the works of the older Anglo-Dutch painters, such as Daniel Mytens and Cornelius Jonson, seem dry and old-fashioned. During the eight years he remained in England, he produced an enormous number of works and established a tradition that later was to form the basis of the great eighteenth-century English school of portrait painting.

Eric Van Schaack

Frans Hals
Dutch, 1580/85-1666

Frans Hals' earliest known dated work is inscribed 1611, and only a few of his paintings, on the basis of stylistic evidence, can be dated around the same time. Thus, the artist (whose birthdate has not been exactly established) was at least twenty-six years old when we first recognize his hand. Where are the works Hals made in his youth or during his early twenties? Are all of them lost? Or was the artist who painted as easily as he breathed a slow starter? The case of Frans Hals' missing juvenilia remains an unsolved mystery.

However, once Hals appears on the scene his spontaneous characterizations and his revolutionary technique are unmistakable. There is no fumbling or groping. This can be seen in his *Pieter Cornelisz van der Morsch,* not a youthful work but one of his earliest existing paintings. The model's vivacious expression and momentary gesture show Hals' radical break with the stiff conventions of early seventeenth-century Dutch portraiture. Even more remarkable is the artist's daring use of detached brush strokes to model form and suggest texture and light, while giving the work an unprecedented pictorial animation. He has already mastered the original technique which he will use during the following fifty years of his long career.

Van der Morsch was well known in Leiden where he was a municipal beadle and won local fame for playing the part of the buffoon in performances arranged by societies of rhetoricians. The fact that Hals painted him holding a smoked herring which he seems to have just taken from his huge straw basket and included the inscription *WIE BEGEERT* (Who Wants It) on the portrait led earlier critics to conclude that the sitter must have been a herring fisherman or a herring merchant. A convincing iconographical analysis of the portrait made by P.J.J. van Thiel (1961) demonstrates that this interpretation of the herring and the motto is incorrect.

Van Thiel's study shows that Hals represented van der Morsch in his role as Piero, the famous Leiden rhetorician and buffoon. He presents ample evidence to prove that in Hals' time the expression "to give someone a smoked herring" had nothing to do with distributing fish but meant to shame someone with a caustic remark or to "give a lick with the rough side of one's tongue." Thus, the inscription *WIE BEGEERT* is not a reference to the sale of herring but to van der Morsch's sharp wit, ever ready to deliver a slap or rebuke.

During the following decades Hals occasionally used other then commonplace sym-

7   PORTRAIT OF PIETER CORNELISZ VAN DER MORSCH, CALLED PIERO
(MAN WITH A HERRING)   1616
Oil on panel, transferred to canvas;
33 1/2 x 26 1/2 inches
Inscribed upper left: *WIE/ BEGEERT*
Inscribed and dated upper right:
AETAT SVAE 73/ 1616
Lent by the Museum of Art, Carnegie Institute

bolic allusions in his commissioned portraits, but the bulk of these pictures were straightforward likenesses seen against neutral backgrounds—even the coats-of-arms disappeared.

Portrait of Vincent Laurensz van der Vinne is an impressive painting of Hals' last phase when the bravura and gaiety of his early works give way to a new restraint and a greater psychological penetration. There is no fundamental change in the aged master's technique, but the paint becomes thinner,

8 PORTRAIT OF VINCENT LAURENSZ
VAN DER VINNE 1655-60
Oil on canvas; 25 1/2 x 19 1/4 inches
Indecipherable monogram lower right
Lent by the Art Gallery of Ontario

his touch more summary. Some strokes gain in breadth and power, while miraculously fine adjustments in the transitional tones fuse others, suggesting the shimmer of silvery light filtering over forms and surfaces. Vivid color accents become rare, and the characteristic monochromatic effect of the deep olive greens and dark grays of this late work is relieved by subtle contrasts of warm and cool colors as well as the fluid brushwork.

Van der Vinne was a painter, draughtsman and poet who belonged to a Haarlem family of artists. The identification of his portrait is based upon his own crude mezzotint after it. Other artists were also fascinated by the portrait; more copies of it are known than of most of Hals' late works. Clearly the French impressionists were not the first artists who studied Hals' technique. They were, however, the first to grasp that it could express a pulsating moment of life animated by sparkling light.

Seymour Slive

Nicolas Poussin
French, 1594-1665

9 MOSES SWEETENING THE WATERS OF MARAH
c.1627-28
Oil on canvas; 60 x 82 1/2 inches
The Baltimore Museum of Art
Gift of Friends of the Museum

Few artists of comparable stature and historic importance have been as slow in maturing as Poussin. Among the *virtuosi* of the seventeenth century, his lack of precociousness is particularly marked. His first teachers were provincial artists of little importance, and he was eighteen or nineteen before he went to Paris. Although he remained there until he was nearly thirty, he accomplished little of lasting importance.

In March of 1624 he arrived in Rome and for several years worked in a variety of styles that reflected the prevailing art currents. During the late 1620's he experimented with the problem of composing paintings with large-scale figures; it is this phase of his early career that can be seen in *Moses Sweetening the Waters of Marah.*

Anthony Blunt has pointed out that the subject (Exodus xv. 22-25) was often cited by early Christian writers as one of the fore-shadowings in the Old Testament of the Christian scheme of salvation (Blunt, 1967, pp. 179-180). The waters were thought to symbolize mankind, corrupted by original sin, and Moses' purification was seen as a prefiguration of the redemption of mankind through the cross of Christ. This subject is extremely rare, and some of the details of the painting, such as Moses placing a stick in the waters instead of a tree, are in agreement with the account of the episode given by Flavius Josephus in his *Jewish Antiquities* (1930 ed., IV, p. 323).

Poussin's interest in the art of the great Venetians of the sixteenth century is particularly marked in this painting with its warm tonalities and free handling. The figures have been organized into a compact group, showing in its spatial organization Poussin's allegiance to certain ideals of pictorial order that characterize the Italian High Renaissance. The

26

10　BAPTISM OF CHRIST　c.1655-57
Oil on canvas; 37 7/8 x 53 3/8 inches
Lent from the John G. Johnson Collection

painting should also be seen as a psychological drama. The idea that the painter should strive to represent emotions through gesture and facial expression was deeply rooted in Italian art theory from the fifteenth century onward. Each character clearly shows his or her response to the miracle, the calm of the elders behind Moses being contrasted with the other observers who register both astonishment and gratitude.

As Poussin grew older, his theoretical preoccupations led him to gradually abandon the more sensual aspects of pictorial art. There is an increase in gravity and dignity which begins in the mid-1640's and becomes more marked during the last decade of the artist's life. The *Baptism of Christ* is characteristic of this final phase of Poussin's career. As in the *Moses,* the figures overlap each other and are arranged in a tightly knit group, but now they are placed in the more clearly articulated space of an idyllic landscape setting. The colors are deliberately muted, and no violent action breaks the somber mood of the painting as the Baptist performs the sacred ritual with quiet solemnity. By this time, Poussin had become one of the most respected artists in Rome, but he remained deliberately aloof from the "official" art world. His late works, executed often for his personal friends, have an almost "puritanical simplicity" (Blunt, 1953, p. 194). Even the eloquent gestures of the earlier pictures have been eliminated in favor of a carefully restrained understatement. Few painters were willing to follow the lead of his severe classicism, but in his patient search for solutions to complex, self-imposed pictorial problems, he has profoundly influenced many artists, among them Cézanne.

Eric Van Schaack

27

Rembrandt van Rijn
Dutch, 1606-69

From the moment nineteen-year old Rembrandt set himself up as an independent Master in his native town of Leiden in 1625, he was determined to make his mark as a painter of biblical subjects. His interest in religious themes never flagged. During the course of his career he did more works based on Scripture than any other subject.

Rembrandt's first efforts in this category show the impact of Pieter Lastman's crowded compositions, surfeited with genre and still life detail. However, as we see in *The Tribute Money* of 1629, he quickly surpassed his teacher by achieving greater concentration and a more intense mood with his chiaroscuro effects: deep shadows suppress details of the crowd and the vast fantastic setting; light has been used to focus attention on the main action. Within the natural light which streams into the great hall a divine light glows. A golden radiance, not a traditional halo, sets apart the Man the huddled Pharisees tried to entangle in His talk: ". . . Master we know that thou art true, and teachest the way of God in truth, neither carest thou for any man: for thou regardest not the person of men. Tell us therefore, what thinkest thou? Is it lawful to give tribute unto Caesar, or not? But Jesus perceived their wickedness, and said, "Why tempt ye me, ye hypocrites? Show me the tribute money. And they brought unto him a penny. And he saith unto them, Whose is this image and superscription? They say unto him, Caesar's. Then saith he unto them, Render therefore unto Caesar the things which are Caesar's; and unto God the things that are God's. When they heard these words they marveled. . ." (Matthew xxii. 16-22).

A pen drawing of an *Oriental Leaning on a Stick* (Benesch, 1954, I, No. 10) has been identified as a study in reverse for the turbaned Pharisee in the foreground, and it is not difficult to imagine that Rembrandt used another study from life for the seated figure on the right who listens to Christ's teaching.

Two or three years after Rembrandt painted *The Tribute Money* he moved to Amsterdam where he soon established his reputation as the leading artist of the United Netherlands. In 1634 he married Saskia van Uylenburgh who bore him four children. Titus, born in 1641, was the only one who survived infancy. The mature Rembrandt painted his son frequently. The *Portrait of Titus* he made in 1660 is an outstanding example of the warm human sympathy, the breadth of handling and the increased

11 THE TRIBUTE MONEY 1629
Oil on panel; 16 3/8 x 12 7/8 inches
Monogrammed and dated
In cartouche, upper right: *RHL • 1629*
Lent by The National Gallery of Canada

power of the chiaroscuro in Rembrandt's late works.

The youth is seen seated in an armchair with his chin resting on his right hand Apparently this was an attitude Titus assumed naturally; when Rembrandt painted him in 1655 seated behind a desk, he showed him in a similar pose (Rotterdam, Boymans-van Beuningen Museum). In the 1660 portrait the effect is a relaxed and casual one. However, it is evident that Rembrandt had second thoughts about how to achieve it. *Pentimenti* can be seen in the hand supporting his chin.

The passage of bright red on Titus' sleeve is the only vivid accent in the predominately deep black and warm brown color harmony.

12 PORTRAIT OF TITUS, THE ARTIST'S SON 1660
Oil on canvas; 32 x 27 inches
Signed and dated on chair back,
right center: *Rembrandt f. 1660*
The Baltimore Museum of Art
The Mary F. Jacobs Collection

As in his early phase the chiaroscuro device remains the master's principle means of pictorial organization, but both the quality and the expressive power of the light and shadow have changed. Although the light is concentrated on Titus' hand and face, we do not sense that a strong beam has been focused upon them. They seem to emerge from the surrounding darkness. In the broadly brushed areas the heavy impasto combined with delicate glazes contributes to a greater surface movement, while an intricate play of half-tones lends a mild vibrant quality to the whole. Intangible elements of light and shadow are now miraculously bound together, creating an atmosphere which not only allows us to share the young man's mood, but appears to be a living substance fluctuating in space.

Seymour Slive

Peter Paul Rubens
Flemish, 1577-1640

Throughout his career Rubens made many copies of other artists' work, following a practice standard at that time in the education of an artist. *Portrait of Mulay Ahmad* (King of Tunis) is just such a copy, painted after a work executed by the Dutch artist, Jan Vermeyen, sometime between 1535 and 1542. The original is now lost, but another copy of it still exists in the form of an etching made by Vermeyen himself (Held, 1940, pp. 173-180).

Julius Held has dated Rubens' portrait around 1609, the year after the artist returned to Antwerp from an eight-year sojourn in Italy. Although thirty-two at this time, Rubens was just beginning to express his full personal style. *Portrait of Mulay Ahmad* is an example of this transitional period, for while it is a study piece and closely follows the original, it displays subtle alterations which mark the painting as something more than a mere reproduction.

Rubens' figure is far more imposing and dignified than Vermeyen's and more natural in its proportions. He eliminates fussy details in the costume and background, focusing attention on the arresting portrait head. Vermeyen had actually met this man who had his father blinded in the process of seizing his throne and in his portrait emphasized the King's individual characteristics; Rubens, however, was more interested in Mulay Ahmad as the representation of a physical type rather than as a specific personality. The face of Rubens' King is more subtle in its expression and more sympathetic than Vermeyen's rendering. Further modified and reinterpreted, Mulay Ahmad reappears as King Balthazar in three of Rubens' renditions of the *Adoration of the Magi* painted between 1609 and 1624.

Portrait of the Archduke Ferdinand was painted shortly after the sitter became Governor of Flanders. The sense of aristocratic grandeur and power which pervades the figure of the King of Tunis is here transplanted and augmented in the figure of the Archduke surrounded by the magnificent trappings of the "grand manner" portrait.

Portrait of Mulay Ahmad bears the imprint of the sixteenth-century mannerist painting which inspired it. The figure is sharply outlined against the far-off background scene which it dominates and from which it appears completely isolated. Frontally presented, the figure forms a stable triangle which nearly fills the canvas. The late *Portrait of the Archduke Ferdinand* is more typically baroque in its spatial construction. Sharp diagonals — resulting from the slight contrapposto of the body, the turning of the

13 PORTRAIT OF MULAY AHMAD   c.1609
Oil on panel; 39 1/2 x 28 inches
Lent by the Museum of Fine Arts, Boston
Maria Theresa Burnham Hopkins Fund

JAN VERMEYEN   (DUTCH, c.1500-59)
Portrait of Mulay Ahmad   c.1535-42
Etching (not included in the exhibition)

head and the angular positioning of arms and elbows — are continued in the drapery and the architectural elements of the background, effecting visual progressions into deep space and firmly linking foreground with the middle distance and background. These forms are stabilized by the manner in which they are distributed on the surface plane of the picture so that energy is checked by order. The amazingly fluid use of brush and pigment and deft placement of light and shadow are far more advanced here than in the earlier portrait, causing forms to flow naturally one out of another and merging all passages into a powerful image of a man who was also a symbol.

Diana F. Johnson

14 PORTRAIT OF THE ARCHDUKE FERDINAND, CARDINAL-INFANTE OF SPAIN 1635
Oil on canvas; 46 1/2 x 37 1/4 inches
Lent by the John and Mable Ringling
Museum of Art

Jacob van Ruisdael
Dutch, 1628/9-82

15 TREES AND DUNES (LANDSCAPE NEAR
DORDRECHT) 1648
Oil on panel; 12 1/2 x 22 1/4 inches
Monogrammed and dated lower right: *JR 1648*
Lent by the Museum of Fine Arts
Springfield, Massachusetts

Jacob van Ruisdael's early painting *Trees and Dunes* is a paraphrase of Rembrandt's famous etching of the *Three Trees* (Hind, 1912, #205). Rembrandt's print is dated 1643; Ruisdael's picture, 1648. The romantic spirit of the etching was in fact exceptional with Rembrandt but struck a highly sympathetic chord in Ruisdael, who in 1649 was to respond to it in one of his own etchings as well. In painting *Trees and Dunes,* he was fascinated by the challenge to translate the romantic mood of the Rembrandt print into his own pictorial language; the rich effect of a pink and yellow sky behind the somber trees in this early work is an almost unique feature in Ruisdael's oeuvre and transcends the quiet use of similar colors found in paintings by his main model, Cornelis Vroom, and by his uncle, Salomon van Ruysdael. The panorama view with one foreground "wing," so brilliantly employed in this picture, is in the same decade often found with Jan van Goyen, and even earlier with Hercules Seghers, either of whom may in fact have inspired Rembrandt's etching in the first place.

The most famous panoramas by Ruisdael were actually painted twenty to twenty-five years later; they, too, are indebted to a Rembrandt print, but this time not to the almost blatantly romantic *Three Trees* but to the much more factual, serene and more subtly constructed *View of Amsterdam* (Hind, 1912, #176), etched almost simultaneously with the *Three Trees.* However, the prototype of the *Waterfall,* which Ruisdael painted in the mid or late sixties, is as far removed from Rembrandt's world as can be imagined. The grandeur of Scandinavian scenery of this kind, with its rushing waters and splendidly erect fir trees, was first discovered by Allaert van Everdingen, who had traveled in Sweden and Norway in 1644 before settling in Haarlem, Ruisdael's home town, the following year. Ruisdael's scenes of this type, usually painted on upright canvases, were universally acclaimed in the nineteenth century. They have lost some of their prestige today, but there is no better way to regain respect and admiration for them than by comparing the finest among them, such as the impeccably preserved example from the Fogg Art Museum, with Everdingen's pioneering but often somewhat poorly organized efforts. In the *Waterfall* everything is placed exactly in the one right spot within the total composition, and there is no crowding and no repetition.

With all its rich splendor and its profoundly romantic mood, this is an art of supreme order and wise economy of means.

One can still hear an echo of the Ruisdael of 1648; both works reflect a romanticism rarely encountered in Dutch seventeenth-century landscape painting. But the work from the master's later period evinces a special quality which, without containing a trace of classicism, may well be termed truly *classical*.

Wolfgang Stechow

16 WATERFALL c.1665
Oil on canvas; 38 3/5 x 33 3/4 inches
Signed lower right: *Ruisdael*
Lent by the Fogg Art Museum, Harvard University
Gift of Miss Helen Clay Frick

Bernardo Strozzi
Italian, 1581-1644

Born in Genoa, Bernardo Strozzi entered in 1596 the studio of Pietro Sorri, a mannerist from Siena. Soon after, he decided to join a Capuchin monastery, but around 1610, in order to support his mother, he left monastic life and devoted himself fully to art. After his mother's death in 1630, he moved to Venice. Recognized as a leading painter in his newly adopted town, Strozzi brought to Venetian painting a new life and freshness and, together with two other outsiders, Domenico Fetti from Rome and Jan Liss from Germany, inaugurated Venetian baroque painting.

The Adoration of the Shepherds, one of Strozzi's most lyrical and serene works, reflects his early connections with the late mannerists, both Italian and Flemish. The impact of Pietro Sorri, of Federico Barrocci, an Umbrian who worked on occasion in Genoa, and of the Florentine mannerists was tempered here by his awareness of the works in Genoa of such Flemish masters as Pieter Aertsen and Joachim Beuckelaer. The extreme delicacy in his handling of the faces, particularly in the youthful representation of the Virgin, and his brilliant brushwork, so masterfully executed in the still life elements and in the figure of the shepherd at right, make this painting an outstanding example of his early Genoese period.

The *Allegory of Sculpture* is a late, more powerful work in which Strozzi reveals his devotion to Veronese. It is a replica of a large *tondo* painting of the same subject which he executed between October 27 and November 27, 1635 for the Biblioteca Marciana in Venice where eighty years earlier Veronese had also worked.

The mannerist features, evident in Strozzi's early works, have been replaced in the *Allegory of Sculpture* by a more monumental, baroque approach. The vigorous forms, the imposing architectural elements, the open sky area and the strong colors are characteristic of his later period. Without losing his personal style, Strozzi revived in such works as this the splendor of the previous century and created the foundation for the development of *Seicento* painting in Venice.

Michael Milkovich

17 THE ADORATION
OF THE SHEPHERDS c.1618-20
Oil on canvas; 38 1/2 x 54 5/8 inches
Lent by The Walters Art Gallery

18 ALLEGORY OF SCULPTURE 1635
Oil on canvas; 76 1/2 x 59 1/2 inches
Lent from the Brandeis University Art Collection

Eighteenth
Century

Canaletto (Antonio Canal)
Italian, 1697-1768

Giovanni Antonio Canal disliked the theater. After only four years of assisting his father and brother in the family enterprise of painting stage scenery, the twenty-two year old Canaletto swore never again to tolerate the fickle whims of impresarios and artists but to devote himself to a related, though more tranquil branch of painting, the *veduta*. The mathematical expertise required to plot the vast illusionistic perspectives of baroque theater design stood him in good stead when it came to depicting his native Venice. A child of the age of reason, he adapted the *camera ottica*, a box device in which a lens cast an image on a ground glass, allowing the painter to compose and to calibrate spatial relationships in preparing his drawings and paintings.

In his earliest views of Venice Canaletto reflects the more romanticized image of the city made popular by the stormy light in the *vedute* of Carlevaris, his great predecessor in this genre of painting. Soon, however, his rational candor replaces drama with a lucid clarity in which blazing light focuses minute detail into an ensemble as fascinating in its microcosmic analysis as it is coherent in its pictorial unity. The *Grand Canal Looking Southwest* is among the earliest examples of this uniquely personal style. Viewed from the lower steps of the Rialto bridge, its topographical description of the houses and palaces along the Canal is a fitting record of the monumental — the imposing Palazzo Grimani in the center distance — and the everyday — merchants unloading produce at the busy Fondamenta del Vin at right. Significantly, it was painted for Joseph Smith who in turn sold it to the Earl of Wicklow in England. Smith made a special career of acting as middleman between Canaletto and the English who carried his pictures home as souvenirs of sunnier days on the Grand Tour.

After more than twenty years of serving English patrons, Canaletto drew on their support in a new and trying situation. In 1741 the Wars of the Austrian Succession had brought tourism to a virtual standstill and with it Canaletto's career. Realist that he was, he determined that if the English could not come to him, he would go to them, and in 1746 he set out for London. With several visits to his native shores to relieve nostalgia, the painter remained in England until shortly

19   VIEW OF VENICE, GRAND CANAL:
LOOKING SOUTHWEST FROM
THE RIALTO TO THE PALAZZO FOSCARI
before 1730
Oil on canvas; 19 1/2 x 28 3/4 inches
Lent by The Museum of Fine Arts, Houston
Robert Lee Blaffer Memorial Collection

20 CAPRICCIO: A PAVILION AND
A RUINED ARCADE BY THE LAGOON   c. 1755
Oil on canvas; 41 1/2 x 41 inches
The Baltimore Museum of Art
The Mary F. Jacobs Collection

after 1755 when he returned to Venice for a belated reception into its Academy and a final decade in which old age reduced his productivity.

It is probable that Canaletto painted the *Capriccio . . .* , here exhibited, in England just after one of his visits home. It belongs to a genre of pictures he painted throughout his life but which was becoming progressively more popular after mid-century: a fanciful compilation of monuments, some purely imaginary and others loosely based on existing buildings, in an unusual landscape or lagoon setting. In this instance the ruined arch recalls the artist's travels to Rome, and the city gate is patterned on those of Padua which he had painted a de-

cade before. Even English garden gothic is amusingly fused with byzantine in the cupola which crowns the gate. Taste had tired of Canaletto's brisk directness and was demanding a nostalgic reverie on departed glory. Such daydreams were inimical to the painter's sharply focused reason and must have evoked memories of the hated theater of his youth. As his subjects became more fanciful, his style became more crisply mechanical. Grand though the architecture may be, it is the reality of the sharp Venetian light, the repeated pattern of white-edged wavelets and the mundane boatmen which catch the eye and fascinate the mind.

Roger Rearick

John Singleton Copley
American, 1737/38-1815

21   PORTRAIT OF JOHN BOURS   1758-61
Oil on canvas; 50 1/4 x 40 1/8 inches
Lent by the Worcester Art Museum
Purchase from the Bequest of
Mrs. Hester Newton Wetherell

There has been a belief among American critics that Copley's art declined after his departure from America, a belief fostered by the fact that until very recently his English period was poorly represented here. Of late years we have either acquired or seen the big subject pictures, *Watson and the Shark, The Death of Chatham, The Death of Major Peirson,* and a number of his English portraits have come to America; but the older conception of his English work still remains with us. The portraits of *John Bours* and *Sir Robert Graham,* therefore, pose a double question, not only of youth and age but of New England and Old England.

When *John Bours* was painted, Copley was in the first flush of success in creating his own form of the rococo portrait of elegance for New England. He faced, however, a problem of character in this subject rare among his New England sitters: a man of retiring habit and devout, inward turning mind. Little is known of Bours' quiet life beyond what Copley and the records of Trinity Church, Newport, tell us. He was born a member of the Church of England gentry of Newport who had built that church; he served as its lay reader for five years, and his name occurs constantly in its records. The young man whom Copley por-

22 PORTRAIT OF SIR ROBERT GRAHAM **1804**
Oil on canvas; 57 1/4 x 46 7/8 inches
Signed left center: *J S Copley. R A. pinx*
Inscribed on envelope: *Mr:/ Baron Graham/ London*
Lent by the National Gallery of Art
Washington, D. C., Gift of Mrs. Gordon Dexter

trays, dressed soberly in brown velvet and snowy linen, is more than a figure of elegance. Copley painted him in an unusual attitude, leaning back in his chair, his pale gentle face absorbed in the thoughts inspired by the book held half-open in his hand. It is an eloquent characterization and unique, or very nearly so, in Copley's work.

The artist was sixty-six and had been nearly thirty years in London when he painted Sir Robert Graham in the robes of a baron of the Exchequer. London was different from Boston: its houses were larger, its life more weighty with rank and cere-

mony. London taste demanded that portraits be effective decorations as well as likenesses. This one shows that Copley had mastered the rich, fluent, decorative qualities of London painting. It demonstrates also that he could paint an official portrait, an image of the authority and self-assurance of a man of high rank and great affairs, no less effectively than one of a quiet New Englander.

We must revise our opinion of Copley's English period. He remained an admirable painter until old age and ill health overtook him.

E. P. Richardson

Jean Honoré Fragonard
French, 1732-1806

No French artist — prior to the impressionists — has ever exposed more eloquently than Fragonard the futility of the time-honored distinction between a *finished painting* and a *sketch*. In his case, these terms become almost irrelevant for, regardless of the degree of Fragonard's *fa presto* exuberance, each one of his works constitutes a highly animated but also coherent statement — pictorially self-sufficient on its own terms.

Fragonard's pictorial logic does not impede in the least his breathtaking virtuosity. However, this expression should not be misconstrued as an indication of superficiality. Frago (a diminutive he liked to sport) is not merely brilliant: his brushwork — his handwriting — is endowed with a lyrical power which colors the meaning of any subject he may choose to depict. This is the quality which is so subtly evoked by Paul de Saint-

23   REST ON THE FLIGHT INTO EGYPT   c.1750
Oil on canvas; 26 x 22 1/2 inches (oval)
The Baltimore Museum of Art
The Mary F. Jacobs Collection

24 THE SACRIFICE OF THE ROSE
(THE OFFERING TO LOVE) 1780-88
Oil on canvas; 13 x 9 3/4 inches
Lent by Wildenstein and Co., Inc.

Victor when he writes that "Fragonard's brushwork recalls the accents which, in certain languages, give to mute words a melodious sound" (Goncourt, 1914, III, p. 278). Fragonard's style is influenced by a great variety of sources ranging from Boucher to Rembrandt, and his themes are as protean as the moods of Diderot's hero in *Le Neveu de Rameau*. Yet, all these heterogeneous elements miraculously coalesce into one of the most individual artistic expressions of the eighteenth century.

The evolution of Fragonard's art is reflected in the confrontation of the two paintings included in the present exhibition. Like most of his religious works, *Rest on the Flight into Egypt* belongs to the early years of his career, and, not too surprisingly, it retains some kinship with the interpretation of the same subject now in the Hermitage by his teacher, Boucher. However, Fragonard's treatment is lighter (the famous *palette de nuage*) and, despite a note of playfulness, his figures have a gently graceful dignity seldom found in Boucher. One thinks of a composition of Murillo, etherealized through the understatements of eighteenth-century technical freedom.

This freedom acquires a new meaning, thirty-odd years later, in *The Sacrifice of the Rose*. In this transparently erotic allegory, the figures lose some of their individual existence to become a part of a total pictorial animation. By-passing the specific definition of form and detail, Fragonard's deceivingly erratic sketchiness finds its *raison d'être* in the strange combination of Dionysian excitement and mysterious intimacy which pervade the subject that recalls *The Fountain of Love* in the Wallace Collection. In this painting, through its hasty linear accents, its uneven impasto and its interplay of delicately faded and vivid hues, Fragonard achieves a fusion of the enigmatic atmosphere of his subject with the elements of form and technique he brings to it. The impetuosity of this conception transcends the decorative brio of the rococo tradition and points to romanticism — and beyond. We are quite far from the gentle charm of *Rest on the Flight*; to paraphrase the Goncourts, in *The Sacrifice of the Rose*, the eighteenth-century erotic theme is transfigured by a St. Theresa-like mystical intensity.

George Levitine

Thomas Gainsborough
British, 1727-88

"English Rococo" sounds a little odd, but is an accurate description of the ornamental landscape style which was developed in England in the 1740's and was probably taught at the St Martin's Lane Academy in London, where Hayman and Gravelot were teaching painting and drawing. Gravelot was a Frenchman, who had been a pupil of Boucher, and it was through him that the Anglicized rococo landscape style was brought about, a style that was made popular by Hayman in the decorations at Vauxhall Gardens in the 1740's. These were the most frequently seen, up-to-date paintings in London in those years when the young Gainsborough was there learning his art. Even though he was not apprenticed to either of them, Hayman and Gravelot were his principal teachers. On the side he also repaired Dutch seventeenth-century landscapes for the art trade. During this time he experimented in two landscape styles: one, the ornamental rococo manner which was also used by professional decorators for overmantles, overdoors and the like; the other, a style based on the direct study of nature seen through the eyes of Dutch landscape painters such as Ruisdael and Wynants. The two styles meet and blend in the *View in Suffolk*. The general pattern of the landscape is akin to rococo stage scenery: a stage sunset makes the rosy sandbanks (which are in the manner of Berghem) glow, but the distant shrubs and trees are observed carefully from the local Suffolk scene. The "shepherd and shepherdess" are artificial figures, but the boy watering a horse is beautifully observed from nature. The sunset is artificial, but the way the light falls is carefully calculated. The date must be in the middle 1750's.

25 VIEW IN SUFFOLK
(RIVER, WITH HORSE DRINKING, . . .) c.1755
Oil on canvas; 37 x 49 1/2 inches
Lent by the City Art Museum of St. Louis

The Harvest Wagon was painted about thirty years later in the winter of 1784-85. The basic motif — a wagon with four horses halted by the wagoner, rustic figures seated at the back and a boy helping a girl to climb in — had been treated some twenty years earlier in a picture now in the Barber Institute, Birmingham, England, in which the landscape is only a pretty backdrop to a figure arrangement derived from Rubens. The Toronto picture is the most artfully evolved of all Gainsborough's later landscapes, in which figures and trees and slopes are blended together in a swirling movement of beautifully orchestrated complexity.

We can see in this painting what Gainsborough meant, writing in 1767, when he says that the figures in a landscape should only "fill a place (I won't say stop a gap) or create a little business for the eye to be drawn from the trees in order to return to them with more glee." We can also see how much he had studied Rubens and Watteau to create an entirely novel and personal style of his own. The early *View in Suffolk* is an individual variant, of great charm, on a style that was widely current, if not hackneyed; the late picture is a perfect realization of a consistent world of the painter's own creation. The play of light and the liking for the time of sunset is common to both. In *The Harvest Wagon* the last rays of the setting sun illumine the face of the wagoner and the figures in the back of the cart, and give hints of a crepuscular poetry, a tinge of sadness, which Gainsborough has in common with Watteau, a painter he is known to have revered.

Ellis Waterhouse

26 THE HARVEST WAGON 1784-85
Oil on canvas; 48 x 59 inches
Initialed lower center: *T. G.*
Lent by the Art Gallery of Ontario
Gift of Mr. and Mrs. Frank P. Wood, 1941

Fancisco José de Goya y Lucientes
Spanish, 1746-1828

The art of Goya is as protean as that of his compatriot Picasso, but unlike the latter, Goya was no child prodigy astounding his teachers and confreres with the results of an early talent. His unique and stupendous genius did not manifest itself until his recovery in 1793 from a grave illness which left him deaf.

Recently scholars such as Gudiol (1964, pp. 13-17) have ascertained that several paintings and a number of murals, which Goya executed between 1773-74 for churches in and near Saragossa, already contain the fundamental elements that distinguish the famous "black pictures" which he created in his old age for his House of the Deaf Man. The answer to the question whether these beginnings anticipate the master's final achievements must be left to the experts. Whatever their conclusions may be, the fact remains that the bulk of Goya's early output consisted of portraits and the cartoons for the Royal Tapestry Manufactory — commissions which preoccupied him from 1775 to 1780 and again from 1786 to 1791. These works are predominantly rococo in spirit — facile, often elegant and whimsical, produced in the artistic language of the cosmopolitan eighteenth century but with a definite Spanish accent. *A Maja with Two Toreros* belongs to the first series of the tapestry designs. Because of their three-dimensional quality, these cartoons were not particularly suited for translation into the tapestry medium but, if evaluated as paintings, they are enchanting in their freshness, verve and rare combination of folklore and sophistication. Goya may have found the inspiration for works such as *A Maja with Two Toreros* in the decorations of North Italian villas by the Tiepolos, and he may have followed Boucher's example in painting the landscape like the backdrop of a stage set, but he relied on his heritage and his own inventiveness in conceiving the subject of this picture, in fixing the stance of each figure, in treating the textures and choosing the colors.

This type of playful genre scene, so characteristic of Goya's early output, disappeared from his oeuvre after 1793, the year of his near fatal illness that mysteriously activated the tremendous scope of his creativity. The following two decades witnessed Goya's phenomenal rise to fame; they also included his passionate love affair with the Duchess of Alba and her early death, the horrors of the Franco-Spanish War and the endless political upheavals — events which are reflected in his art.

The last phase of Goya's stylistic evolution found its most poignant expression in the

27   A MAJA WITH TWO TOREROS
(CONFIDENCES IN A PARK)   1779-80
Oil on canvas; 72 1/8 x 39 3/8 inches
Lent by The Museum of Fine Arts, Houston
Samuel H. Kress Collection

28 THE TOPERS 1819
Oil on canvas; 39 7/8 x 31 1/2 inches
Inscribed upper center: MEDIC[O]
Collection mark lower right: 127
Lent by the North Carolina Museum of Art
Gift of the Mary Reynolds Babcock Foundation

works he carried out for himself — the print series of the mysterious *Disparates* (first published thirty-five years after his death) and the nightmarish pictures with which in 1819 he covered the walls of his house. The subject matter of these almost monochrome murals eludes logical explanation; in concept and execution they announce twentieth-century expressionism.

Of approximately the same date as the "black pictures" of the House of the Deaf Man, *The Topers* is related to them in its muted tonality, its sardonic mood and the ugliness of the grimacing faces with their mindless grins and mouths agape. However, the strong chiaroscuro and the emphasis on contour set this work apart as does its subject which recalls the iconography of Frans Hals and his school, though Goya's rendering is more savagely grotesque than that of any Dutch seventeenth-century painter.

Except for some of the highlights put on with the palette knife, the paint appears rather fluid and rapidly applied — sometimes with brush strokes which do not seem to define shapes realistically. Nevertheless, Goya has evoked three-dimensional form by his unique manipulation of volume and light. Certain areas of the painting are reminiscent of Velazquez' treatment of textures; the pictorial beauty of these passages sharply contrasts with the debased faces of the two men.

Because of the large inscription *MEDICO* in the background, it has been assumed that *The Topers* was a gift from the artist to his physician Arrieta who treated him during a serious illness in 1819 and whom Goya depicted in 1820 in the *Self Portrait with Dr. Arrieta* inscribed with his expression of gratitude to his friend for having saved his life.

G. R.

Jean Baptiste Greuze
French, 1725-1805

The name of Greuze is usually associated with the saccharine sentimentalism and the furtive eroticism which permeate his elaborately pantomimed lessons of domestic virtue and transparent allegories. These qualities are invariably brought forth in most discussions of Greuze's art, with a traditional criticism of the porcelain-like texture of his paintings and a traditional reference to the excessive praise given to him in Diderot's *Salons*.

Whatever its merit, this characterization fails to take into account the surprising trends which occur in Greuze's portraiture. Thus, the *Portrait of the Marquise de Besons* seems to show more kinship with the productions of the fashionable eighteenth-century portrait specialists, such as Nattier and Roslin, than with Greuze's much more "typical" picture *The Rest* with which it was exhibited in the Salon of 1759. However, one should avoid replacing one label by another. Despite the sitter's vacuous *sourire spirituel*, the pastel color scheme, the cascading lace and the other elements conspicuously inspired by the modish Louis Quinze staging, the *Marquise de Besons* is anything but a run-of-the-mill illustration of the rococo recipe. The well-known, eighteenth-century formula is enlivened by Greuze's compositional resourcefulness (use of boldly contrasted isosceles triangles), his exquisite sense of color (subtly different salmon pinks), his epicurean feeling for pigmented surfaces (textured with a slightly buttery impasto), and his inherent lucidity (the details, never elusive, are ordered into well-defined planes). This style, not usually associated with Greuze, cannot be explained by a mere reference to the early date of the work. Greuze's *Marquise de Chauvelin*, painted in 1765, reveals similar qualities and differs in the same manner from the more "typical" *The Ungrateful Son* (Louvre) of that same year, thus closely paralleling the earlier contrast between the *Marquise de Besons* and *The Rest*. Paradoxically, the painter, spurred by the problem of conveying his sitter's physical presence in terms of a socially and stylistically appropriate image, can display an inventiveness which is seldom exemplified in his more ambitious productions of history and genre subjects.

However, in a much later work, the *Portrait of Comtesse Mollien as a Child*, Greuze places reliance on the well-tried approach he so often used in his once popular allegorical *têtes d'expression*, such as *Innocence* (Wallace Collection, London). The fluid outlines, the ceramic density of some passages and the arbitrarily ruffled sketchiness of

29 PORTRAIT OF ANNE-MARIE BAZIN, MARQUISE DE BESONS c.1758
Oil on canvas; 37 x 30 inches
Inscribed upper left: *ANNE MARIE DE BRICQUEVILLE DE LALUSERNE/ EPOUSE DE JACQUES BAZIN MARQUIS DE BESONS/ TRES HAUT ET TRES PUISSANT SEIGNEUR DES/ MAISONS HUPIN NEUVILL, ET AUTRE LIEUX, ET/ LIEUTENANT GENERAL DES ARMEES DU ROI*
The Baltimore Museum of Art
The Mary F. Jacobs Collection

30 PORTRAIT OF COMTESSE MOLLIEN AS
A CHILD 1791
Oil on canvas; 24 5/8 x 19 1/2 inches (oval)
Inscribed on label on stretcher: *ce petit portrait
est le mien, a l'age de six ans et demi,/ fait par
Greuze en 1791./ Adele Dutilleul, Comtesse
Mollien*
The Baltimore Museum of Art
Gift of the William Randolph Hearst Foundation
In Memory of William Randolph Hearst

other areas point to an adroitness acquired through long practice. Yet, the painter is not totally unaware of new trends. The ivory whites, the cool grays and the acid blues echo the neo-classical restraint in regard to color. The sitter's expression is delicately reflective — the effect of teary *sensibilité* begins to yield to pre-romantic pensiveness. Facing the growing success of the classical-romantic portraits of Gérard and Girodet, the aging Greuze is still trying to capture the fashionable pose of the day by following, in his disarmingly charming way, the advice he once gave to a young painter: "try to be *piquant* if you cannot be truthful" (Goncourt, 1914, II, p. 14).

George Levitine

49

Francesco Guardi
Italian, 1712-93

31 VENICE: CHURCH OF SANTA MARIA
DELLA SALUTE c.1750
Oil on canvas; 36 1/4 x 51 3/4 inches
The Baltimore Museum of Art
The Mary F. Jacobs Collection

In 1913 the Venetian scene *Church of Santa Maria della Salute* and its companion piece *The Grand Canal, Venice* were acquired by Mrs. Mary Frick Jacobs as autograph works by Francesco Guardi. This attribution was changed in 1948 when the paintings were ascribed to Michele Marieschi (1710-1744), another Venetian view painter, as the result of Professor W. G. Constable's valid discovery that they were based on two of Marieschi's etchings published in 1741. The paintings were returned, however, to Guardi's authorship in 1965 by Rodolfo Pallucchini, internationally recognized authority on eighteenth-century Venetian painting, who declared them to be very early examples (perhaps the earliest known) of Guardi's *vedute*. Dating them about 1750, he thus corrected the prevailing assumption that Guardi at that time still was active exclusively as a figure painter in the workshop of his older brother Gianantonio.

Pallucchini forcefully stated this opinion in an article in *Arte Veneta* (1966, p. 316). His convincing arguments are based on stylistic evidence, with emphasis on the rendering of the figures that enliven both scenes. These groups do not correspond to those in Marieschi's prints but are original inventions "of the finest quality, already revealing Guardi's free brush stroke and nervous touch." The fact that, aside from the figure groups, the paintings are copies — with only minor modifications — of Marieschi's prints "corroborates the thesis that Francesco Guardi, at the moment when he changed from a figure painter to a view painter based himself above all on the experience of Marieschi, . . . although the execution of the Baltimore pictures follows a different pictorial tradition." Noticing the absence of "those broken-up and residue-like impastos dear to Marieschi," Pallucchini recognizes the overall brownish tonality, the handling of light and the fluid paint quality of the two scenes as characteristic of Francesco. Other observers may realize that "the wavering black outlines of the buildings" mentioned as typical of his *vedute* style (Levey, 1959, p. 98) are already visible here.

Guardi's reinstatement as the painter of the Baltimore *vedute* rightfully is considered "an important discovery" (Zampetti, 1967, p. 296). While pointing out his dependence on Marieschi's prints, these works at the same time reveal Francesco's complete mastery of a highly individual figure style, thus casting light on this aspect of the artist's development about which so little is known.

Although some events of Francesco

32 GRAND CANAL WITH THE CHURCH OF
SANTA MARIA DELLA SALUTE
AND THE DOGANA 1780's
Oil on canvas; 16 1/2 x 26 inches
Lent by the Columbia Museum of Art
Samuel H. Kress Collection

Guardi's later years were recorded as were various commissions he received, on the whole, factual information on his life and work is so scarce that most of his paintings cannot be dated exactly but have been ascribed to certain periods according to stylistic criteria. The beginning of his late style is usually placed after the mid-1770's when his actual views of Venice became increasingly ephemeral, looking more and more like imaginary scenes. Excepting his Marieschi imitations, Guardi was always more of an interpreter than a topographer of his city, but never was he more successful in recreating the many moods, the dream-like quality, the sparkle of Venice than in the works of his old age.

In conception and execution the small picture *Grand Canal with the Church of Santa Maria della Salute and the Dogana* is an excellent example of Guardi's late manner. Probably upon his customers' requests Guardi painted the *Salute* many times; however, there are only very few versions that have as complex a composition as the Columbia painting and equal it in its poetic reality. The frontal view of the *Salute* presented in the early Baltimore picture is here replaced by a side view that emphasizes the island character of the scene. The large, heavy buildings in the middle ground seem to have lost their earth-bound, static existence and, not unlike a mirage, appear to hover over the waters. The dark foreground is relieved by the gently moving gondolas that leave ripples of shimmering light in their train. Michael Levey has called the artist's small late paintings "flickering enchantments" and described the figures in such pictures as "mere specks of color, a running squiggle of white paint, a black dot . . ." (1959, p. 102).

Earlier in this century Guardi was often claimed to have anticipated impressionism. This kinship could easily be felt because of certain properties of his style: his mastery in rendering the Venetian atmosphere, the spontaneity of his brush stroke, the sketch-like nature of his late works and his uncanny ability to evoke an impression of his city. In recent years art historians have rejected any similarities between Guardi's dazzling scenes and impressionist paintings, arguing correctly that the approach of the eighteenth-century painter differed drastically from that of the impressionists. However, remembering Guardi's magnificent Munich canvas which repeats the vista of the Columbia painting but shows the scene at nightfall, one cannot help but think of Monet recording the effects of changing light on his subject matter.

G. R.

Alessandro Magnasco
Italian, 1667-1749

In the ranks of artistic eccentrics Alessandro Magnasco occupies a modest but not uninteresting place. Too little is known of his career, his travels, his patrons and his personality to afford us a clear view of his erratic course through the world of late baroque Italy. His paintings, until this century lost in the backwater of taste, allow us the only access to his temperament. Caustic and redolent of decay, they strike a note of futile irrationality which has found a sympathetic audience in our own day.

When Magnasco was a youth in Genoa, few painters could remember the lively years in which Rubens and van Dyck had worked there. Among local masters Strozzi had long since emigrated to Venice and died, and Castiglione's death had ended a sunny era of classic pastorales. Commerce was slow, the aristocracy parsimonious and commissions to painters few and niggardly. Such was the poverty of the Genoese artistic tradition that Magnasco had to move to Milan for training. There, prospects were scarcely brighter, and he soon settled into practice as a landscapist earning a meager livelihood.

Wooded Landscape with Monks, painted during a six year sojourn in Florence, is in the unkempt tradition of Salvator Rosa. The foreground is dominated by a great tree which illustrates Magnasco's approach to nature in microcosm: scraggly, blasted and overgrown with parasitical vines, it barely survives the cruel forces of nature. Monks, favorite props in Magnasco's paintings, are presented in various states of poverty, despair and drunkenness. By turns ribald and repentant, impoverished and greedy, they share the bleak and angry frustration of their

33 WOODED LANDSCAPE WITH MONKS c.1710
Oil on canvas; 37 x 48 1/4 inches (oval)
Lent by the Dayton Art Institute

setting. In his hands the romantic landscape, already a worn cliché in Italy, was given a rough new vigor.

Magnasco's favored themes — mocking peasants living in ruins, Harlequin and Columbine grown to crones by a dying fire, lunatic clergy conducting grotesque burials, mysterious Jews in gloomy synagogues — remained constant through his more than fifty years of activity. Toward the end of his life subjects such as the *Baptism of Christ,* the *Calling of the Apostles* or simple shipwrecks evince a new interest in the expressive possibilities of maritime settings. Always potentially menacing, nature turns violent in such late pictures as *Bay with Shipwreck.* Figures, disparate in scale, struggle at nonexistent chores; sea, sky and trees are whipped into a seething solution; swans and boatless sails skim a phantom tide; a bridge of colossal proportions looms on the horizon; and waves break with the fury of an atomic explosion. Magnasco has gone from the calculated drama of dark mass and light-shot blueish distance in the early picture to an irrational disorder in which paint is slashed onto the canvas with an energy that no longer relates to the form it is intended to describe. A dissolving chaos, pictorial as well as conceptual, threatens to engulf the form, leaving only the energy of the act of painting to carry its expression to the viewer. It is, perhaps, this aspect of Magnasco's art which speaks most directly to modern taste.

Roger Rearick

34   BAY WITH SHIPWRECK   after 1735
Oil on canvas; 45 1/4 x 68 1/8 inches
Lent by the North Carolina Museum of Art
Samuel H. Kress Collection

Charles Willson Peale
American, 1741-1827

Among the works of Charles Willson Peale there is an exceptional group of pictures created to stand distinct from the many commissioned paintings and the fondly conceived family portraits. These are the "exhibition pieces" of which both *Rachel Weeping* and the *Self Portrait: In the Character of a Painter* are two of the finest.

Peale was always a didactic humanist, and painting was one vehicle which he employed throughout his life to express his sentiments. The "exhibition pieces" were painted both to illustrate Peale's technical accomplishments and to state in unequivocal terms his credo that factual representation is the highest form of art.

In 1766 Peale traveled to London and studied for some two years in Benjamin West's "American School." From this experience he returned to America with the firmly grounded conviction that, above all, painting should convey the illusion of reality. As Charles Coleman Sellers has pointed out (1952, p. 9) the continuation in America of the realistic English portrait tradition ". . . fitted Peale's practical approach to his work and his Deist philosophy." For Peale there was no distinction between Nature and God. Thus, in his painting as well as in his occupation as a naturalist, he strove to illuminate the essence of God through the faithful depiction of both Nature and Man.

While Peale's basic approach to art never altered, while the objectives of painting remained for him fixed upon natural representation, his style of painting changed and matured considerably. His early work is quite linear. Many of the portraits seem to be conceived as line drawings filled in with color. By the late 1770's, however, one begins to detect a more painterly approach. Outlines begin to soften, brushwork becomes freer, and especially in the portraits of women there becomes apparent a more relaxed relationship between the painter and his subjects.

Rachel Weeping illustrates the early Peale at his best. Although this is a tragically serene picture, it is charged with dramatic emotion. It is one of Peale's most singular technical achievements, relying upon a subtle handling of tone and light to convey the intended sentiment without falling into the mistake of sugary overstatement. Until the appearance of the luminist landscapes in the nineteenth century, it is difficult to find in American painting another picture in which tonality is so well handled to create mood and atmosphere. Peale began *Rachel Weeping* in 1772 as a record of the death

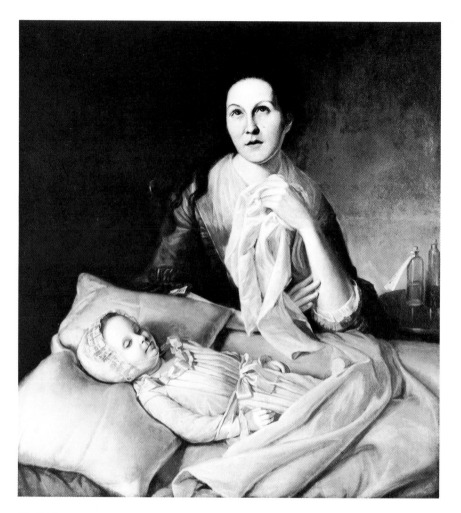

35 RACHEL WEEPING 1772
Oil on canvas; 37 1/8 x 32 1/4 inches
Lent by Charles Coleman Sellers
Courtesy of the
Munson-Williams-Proctor Institute

of his young daughter and in 1776 added the figure of Rachel, his first wife. The picture was given a higher finish around 1818 through glazing techniques developed by Peale's son, Rembrandt.

Self-Portrait: In the Character of a Painter represents the octogenerian still at the height of his artistic powers. The difference between *Rachel Weeping* and the *Self Portrait* is the difference between striving and assurance. The excellence of *Rachel Weeping* is an exception among Peale's work of the 1770's. The excellence of the *Self Portrait* is the rule of Peale's work of the 1820's.

We know from his writings that Peale intended the *Self Portrait* to stand as a demonstration piece, illustrating for other artists both his own technical ability and the artistic heights which the art of portraiture might attain. Thus, he set himself the difficult task of portraying himself in full face view with reflected back light. The lighting is just as dramatic as in *Rachel Weeping,* but the brushwork is freer and more assured than in his paintings prior to 1800. The long-handled brush stands as a symbol of Peale's vocation as a painter and also serves as an important compositional element paralleling the diagonal movement of the left shoulder. Both technically and artistically, this is one of Peale's most ambitious and successful works in which he solved the difficult problems which he continued to set for himself even in his old age.

There is a companion piece to the *Self Portrait: In the Character of a Painter.* It was painted in the same year, 1824, and carries the title *Self Portrait: For the Multitude.* These were Peale's last self portraits, and of them he wrote to his daughter-in-law, Mrs. Rubens Peale, "The painters will admire that [portrait] painted in the reflected light, but the multitude will like the other better. . ." There is no question that Peale valued most highly the respect of his fellow painters. It is just as characteristic, however, that his devotion to public intelligence should have required him to please the multitude as well.

John A. Mahey

36 SELF PORTRAIT:
IN THE CHARACTER OF A PAINTER 1824
Oil on canvas; 26 x 22 inches
Lent by The Pennsylvania Academy
of the Fine Arts

Giovanni Battista Piazzetta
Italian, 1682-1754

Among his playful rococo contemporaries Piazzetta strikes a note of sober baroque grandeur. His early training with the mediocre Antonio Molinare in Venice was supplemented, from about 1703, by an extended stay in the Bolognese studio of Giuseppe Maria Crespi where he learned fluent brushwork, rich impasto, warmly resonant color and dramatic chiaroscuro. He was a patient worker, and although even his largest canvases seem brilliantly spontaneous, he prepared them with deliberate care. After exploring ideas in a few drawings from life, he usually made a rapid oil sketch, the *bozzetto,* in which general relationships of color, form, light and shadow were set down. The next stage was a *modeletto,* a small scale oil in which the character of the projected painting could be worked out in much of its detail. From there began the transfer to altar, mural or ceiling in which the original concept came to its full-blown realization.

Perhaps the first major commission accorded Piazzetta on his return from Bologna to his native Venice was *St. James Led to*

37   ST. JAMES LED TO MARTYRDOM   c.1717
Oil on canvas; 16 7/8 x 13 3/8 inches
Lent Anonymously

38 THE ASSUMPTION OF THE VIRGIN 1743-44
Oil on canvas; 28 1/8 x 15 1/8 inches
Lent by The Cleveland Museum of Art

Martyrdom, one of eleven altarpieces ordered in 1717 from the foremost Venetian artists for the church of S. Stae. With its powerful countermovement, golden color and pungent naturalism, Piazzetta's contribution outshone the work of his older and more famous colleagues, as did that of the still younger Tiepolo. Its vigor is suggested in miniature in the fresh and improvisational *bozzetto* here exhibited. The massive figures of the robust old man and his bronzed assailant loom large on a foreground hillock behind which the ground slopes precipitously away to afford a glimpse of a horseman of the execution party at the lower left. With a masterful shorthand the painter suggests the brusque faith of the indomitable Saint and the pugnacious force of his tormentor.

For almost forty years Piazzetta remained a firm outpost of the baroque in the midst of the growing frivolity of Venice, the playground of Europe. His fame spread through Europe and requests for his paintings came from distant parts of the continent. Among such orders was the commission for *The Assumption of the Virgin,* a large altarpiece he painted in 1744 for the Koenigsaal in Prague. The genesis of this work is documented by the *modeletto* in this exhibition. It is evidence of the artist's unwavering devotion to the principles learned in his youth; it also intimates that to some extent he was influenced by the lightness and delicacy of the younger generation. Although the figures are still impressive in physical presence and grand gesture, they are now more lightly constructed and move with a nervous buoyancy. The sudden contrast of blazing light against melancholy shadow is here modulated to a more even, placid illumination. The familiar lustrous whites, dense blues and dominant cinnamon-rust colors persist, but now in an agitated counterpoint of paler hues.

Belatedly Piazzetta recognized the possibilities of the rococo, but he never abandoned the majestic sobriety of his early style. When he died in 1754 at the age of seventy-one, a relic of a then remote era, the rococo itself was past its apogee. Within a generation the proponents of a doctrinaire neoclassicism would push him into an oblivion from which he has been rescued only in this century with the recognition that, as a figure painter, he is second only to Tiepolo among Italians of his time.

Roger Rearick

Joshua Reynolds
British, 1723-92

Reynolds spent the years from 1750 to 1752 in Rome and absorbed an astonishing amount of the classical and renaissance traditions. He came back to London with a general idea — sometimes considered a gimmick — that was to serve him for the rest of his life and which provides a thread of continuity between his early and his late portraits. This idea was to present the living in poses long made familiar from notable works of art of the past. The appeal is often to an almost subconscious visual tradition, and Reynolds came to use it with an increasing sophistication. In *Portrait of Miss Henrietta Edgcumbe,* painted three years after he had settled in London, this resource is used without any attempt at concealment. The classical motif of the *Kanephoroi* — girls carrying baskets in procession — is perhaps more abundantly familiar today than it was in the eighteenth century, but it was even then something of a cliché of ancient art, and Reynolds has copied his source almost literally, even to the draped stole which probably the sitter never wore. But as a private commission it remains an unpretentious likeness and a charming picture, without any of the pomposity which Reynolds used for his "Exhibition Portraits" (such as the *Lady Stanhope* of 1765 in The Baltimore Museum of Art collection). The slightly faded silvery tone is a characteristic of early Reynolds portraits which has to some extent only developed with the passage of time, but something of the sort seems to have been intended in these early paintings.

Reynolds never went back to Italy; he does not even seem to have wanted to do so. But in 1781 he made a short tour of the Netherlands, where he was particularly impressed by Rubens, whose work was not one of the earlier influences on his art. The prevailing ruddy tone of *Portrait of Sophia, Lady St. Asaph, and Her Son,* and also the bravura of the handling, owe a good deal to Rubens. The baroque trappings, with column and curtain, are a part of the "Exhibition Portrait" style, and the painting was in fact shown at the Royal Academy in 1787. The source of the pattern is much less obvious here than in *Miss Henrietta Edgcumbe.* The upper part of the lady and the child she is holding probably derive from an Italian baroque picture (perhaps a Guido Reni) of *Salome with the Head of the Baptist.* The model would have been a standing figure; as Lady St. Asaph is seated, the lower half of this figure (a good deal of its incongruity concealed by shadow) had to be extemporized. The child, too, may well

39 PORTRAIT OF
MISS HENRIETTA EDGCUMBE   1756
Oil on canvas; 30 1/8 x 25 inches
Lent by the Museum of Fine Arts, Boston
Bequest of Mrs. Robert Dawson Evans

have been taken from an Infant Moses. What is surprising is that a tender and domestic quality of feeling manages to survive all this cookery. Reynold's artistic temperament matured very early; and his feeling for human character — perhaps helped by his deafness — remained constant. What impresses us, as it impressed Gainsborough, is his variety, and his late works are virtuoso variations on his earlier style.

Ellis Waterhouse

40 PORTRAIT OF SOPHIA,
LADY ST. ASAPH, WITH HER SON 1787
Oil on canvas; 55 3/4 x 43 1/2 inches
The Baltimore Museum of Art
Jacob Epstein Collection

Gilbert Stuart
American, 1755-1828

41 PORTRAIT OF CALEB WHITEFOORD 1782
Oil on canvas; 30 x 25 inches
Lent by The Montclair Art Museum

When Gilbert Stuart painted the *Portrait of Caleb Whitefoord* in London, the young artist had just emerged from the naivete of his youthful style and was working easily, for the first time, in the large decorative manner of London. The rich, fluent use of paint, the remote dignity and monumental quality of the portrait are the closest Stuart ever came to the style of Reynolds or Romney.

It is not a penetrating characterization. Whitefoord was a Scottish wine merchant whose wit and literary tastes made him welcome in all circles of London's artistic and literary life. He was at the same time the friend of Dr. Benjamin Franklin, his neighbor on Craven Street, and of the arch-tory Dr. Johnson, a feat which suggests the reasoning behind the British ministry's choice of him as intermediary in the peace negotiations with Franklin in Paris to end the American war. Although Stuart painted him at the moment of those negotiations, he gives us no sense that we are looking at a wit, a pamphleteer, a patron of artists and a man of agile mind and quick sympathies. It is a grave, remote portrait, dark in tone. Stuart, I feel, was intent on showing that he could paint a "great gentleman" as well as could Sir Joshua Reynolds.

In his later years Stuart created a type of neo-classic portrait marked by the same still, remote dignity; but he laid aside the heavy paint, the broad brush stroke and the deep tonality of his London years for a more compact image, a crisper outline, a cleaner and brighter color. Like all his later work, his *Portrait of Mrs. Upham* is marked by a charming luminosity. One sees little change in that style during the last thirty years of Stuart's career. He gave his sitters repose and dignity, sometimes — as is the case with Mrs. Upham — an attractive vitality. But he never wished, or was not interested, to pierce through the *persona* to the flux and play of private feeling which gives individuality to a moment of life. In this respect his art remains constant.

E. P. Richardson

42 PORTRAIT OF
MRS. THOMAS COGSWELL UPHAM c.1825
Oil on canvas; 29 3/4 x 25 3/4 inches
Lent by the Bowdoin College Museum of Art

Giovanni Battista Tiepolo

Italian, 1696-1770

Giovanni Battista Tiepolo is the golden boy of the eighteenth century. Called "the celebrated Tiepolo" in 1726 when he was but thirty, his pictures were given a place of honor in the greatest collections of his day. His service was sought by most of the crowned heads of Europe, and long periods were spent away from his native Venice making frescoes for palaces in Würzburg, Madrid and other cosmopolitan centers. His art remains the epitome of a century of sophistication and virtuosity. And yet Tiepolo began life in a crumbling city better known for its licentious *dolce vita* than for an impoverished artistic tradition, living parasitically on the distant glories of the Renaissance.

Tiepolo's training was in large measure due to his independent and inquisitive study of his artistic patrimony, in particular the sumptuous paintings of Veronese. Endowed with a connoisseur's eye for quality, he was also stimulated by the achievements of his contemporaries who, at the time young Giambattista set up his own shop at about the age of eighteen, had begun to stir from the torpor of the preceding century. Piazzetta especially attracted him with his dramatic chiaroscuro and rich impasto. He joined this distinguished master in adding a picture of his own to the crucial series of eleven pictures painted for the Venetian church of S. Stae. In it, and in the intimate *Susanna and the Elders* painted about the same time, he shows not only his debt to Piazzetta but his peculiarly vivid and personal style as well. The virtuous Susanna is depicted at the moment when the pair of lewd old men surprise her at her bath. She rejects the importunate offer of jewels with a recoiling gesture which combines a forceful baroque diagonal with a plump form and a delicate elegance of undulant line. The drama is emphasized by deep shadow and flickering highlights as in the grasping hands of the elders. These are keyed to the almost animate counterbalance of the triton fountain at right and the touches of vibrant color in the flowers and jewels. Tiepolo's composition is coordinated by a gently breathing continuity of line, richly plastic light and shade, textural variety and a color range almost too fruity in its luscious plum, pink, cerulean blue and creamy white juxtapositions. Exuberant to the edge of vulgarity, *Susanna and the Elders* delights with its high spirits and youthful charm.

Almost forty years later Giambattista was on the eve of his fateful journey to Madrid when he turned to two episodes from the loves of the gods: *Apollo and Daphne*, now

43 SUSANNA AND THE ELDERS c.1718-20
Oil on canvas; 22 x 17 inches
Lent by the Wadsworth Atheneum

44   VENUS AND VULCAN   c.1755-60
Oil on canvas; 26 x 33 1/2 inches
Lent from the John G. Johnson Collection

in the National Gallery of Art, and *Venus and Vulcan* included in this exhibition. After years of covering the ceilings of palaces and churches with cloud banks of gods and saints, lining the walls of villas with ancient histories and embellishing scores of altars with grandiloquent martyrdoms, Tiepolo had evolved a fluent virtuosity unmatched before or since. Perhaps the reticence of this intimate picture provided a welcome opportunity for intensified refinement. It is an essay in tonal variety within a narrow color range; as the *Apollo and Daphne* is dominated by nature colors — forest green, sky blue, sunny gold — the *Venus and Vulcan* is keyed to earth colors — ivory, fawn, russet and bronze. This calculated harmony is matched by a

high-strung formal tension between the angular hauteur of Venus and the counterpull of the diagonally positioned Vulcan, darkly skeptical of his visitor and her portable cloud bank. Arch and nervously self-conscious, the painting is tinged with weariness and prophetic of the galvanic melancholy of his last sketches.

Challenged by the modish neo-classicism of Mengs, Tiepolo saw his last paintings discarded and cut to pieces by his Spanish patrons. His death, which brought a sunny epoch to its conclusion, went unmarked save perhaps by a watchful young Spaniard named Francisco Goya.

Roger Rearick

Elisabeth-Louise Vigée-Lebrun
French, 1755-1842

Madame Vigée-Lebrun, the favorite painter of Marie-Antoinette, was an immensely successful professional portraitist who, above all, was concerned with the rendering of her sitters' likenesses in a manner that would please them most. This particular conception of her speciality is reflected in her works as well as in her writings. For instance, in her "Conseils pour la peinture du portrait" included in her *Souvenirs,* she notes: "The colors of cheeks, if they are natural, must suggest a peach in the receding area, and a golden rose in the protruding one" (1869, II, p. 348). Today, such an approach seems to strike a note of naivete; the very reasons for which this charming woman painter has been so admired during her lifetime (she was occasionally referred to as *Madame van Dyck*) make it difficult to consider her achievements in terms of twentieth-century attitudes toward portraiture.

Yet, Madame Vigée-Lebrun was a highly competent craftsman, and her professional flattery did not prevent her from displaying in her works a sense of coherent composition, a feeling for harmonious color scheme, and a flair for characterization (she prided herself on her talent as a physiognomist). Her sitters retain their individuality, but this individuality is filtered through the fashionable "type" of the period.

Russian models occupy an important place in her considerable portrait gallery. Following the example of some famous Frenchmen, such as Falconet and Diderot, Madame Vigée-Lebrun went to Russia where she spent six years of her wandering life after the fall of the French monarchy; but she cultivated friendly relations with many Russians long before that time, and she executed a number of portraits of Russian aristocrats who often visited Paris during the *ancien régime.*

The *Portrait of Count Shuvaloff* and the *Portrait of Princess Anna Alexandrovna Galitzin* capture two different phases of the emotional climate of the last quarter of the eighteenth century, the period to which Vigée-Lebrun's artistic development was limited. The early portrait reflects the optimistic benevolence and the openheartedness which characterize *l'homme sensible* at the beginning of the reign of Louis XVI, while the later one echoes the classicizing posturing and the dreamy languidness which, around 1800, are sported by the fashionable sufferers of the oncoming *mal du siècle.* The *Count Shuvaloff* is reminiscent of Greuze (i.e. the *Portrait of Wille* in the Jacquemart-André Museum). But Greuze's solidity of

45 PORTRAIT OF COUNT SHUVALOFF 1775
Oil on canvas; 33 x 24 inches (oval)
Lent by the North Carolina Museum of Art

modeling and his porcelain-like density are sacrificed for the sake of a vivacity and a painterly spontaneity which could have resulted from Madame Vigée-Lebrun's contact with Briard and Doyen, the early champions of "dramatic Rubenism." The sources of the *Princess Galitzin* are more evident: the portrait is directly related to a type exemplified by David's *Madame de Verninac* (Louvre). Yet, Madame Vigée-Lebrun does not quite achieve the sculptural strength and the linear purity of the neo-classical conception. She is not quite at ease in this new stylistic context, and she adorns her sitter with a vaguely oriental, variegated attire which allows her to indulge in a complex interplay of transparencies and reflections for which she had already been praised during Marie-Antoinette's era.

George Levitine

46   PORTRAIT OF PRINCESS
ANNA ALEXANDROVNA GALITZIN   1796
Oil on canvas; 54 x 40 inches
The Baltimore Museum of Art
The Mary F. Jacobs Collection

Benjamin West
American, 1738-1820

Benjamin West's *Self Portrait,* with its air of debonair self-assurance, shows the American-born artist early in his very successful London career. Evidently he wanted to be remembered as the painter of *The Death of General Wolfe,* because he has included two figures from that picture in the sketch on the drawing board he holds before him. Undoubtedly West enjoyed the notoriety and acclaim that his famous picture had won. Garrick even imitated the pathetic pose of the dying Wolfe, and West's biographer, the Scottish novelist John Galt, told an elaborate tale about how West's judgment, which led him to show the soldiers in modern uniform, had triumphed over Sir Joshua Reynolds' belief that all military heroes should be painted in classical costumes.

The picture of Wolfe was well known as early as March 1770, although it was not exhibited until 1771 (Chamberlin, 1910, p. 55). So, this *Self Portrait* probably shows West at the age of thirty-two or thirty-three, proud of having caused a stir in the London art world. The portrait also shows that West had learned his lessons very well during his stay in Italy, 1760-63. It seems almost impossible that this very suave, cultured gentle-

47   SELF PORTRAIT   c.1771
Oil on canvas; 29 1/2 x 25 inches
Lent by Mr. and Mrs. Jacob Blaustein

48   BELISARIUS AND THE BOY   1802
Oil on canvas; 26 1/2 x 18 3/4 inches
Signed and dated on stone seat, lower right:
B West/ 1802
Inscribed upper right: *MOENIA VRBIS/*
REPARATA/ SVB IVSTINIANO/ A BELISARIO
Inscribed on plaque, left center: *DAT [...]/*
BELISARIO
Lent by The Detroit Institute of Arts
Gift of A. Leonard Nicholson

man could ever have known the rough life of the American frontier west of Philadelphia or that his first paintings were the work of an untrained primitive. As the portrait indicates, seven years after he had settled in London he had developed a capable handling of paint that reveals a good knowledge of the widely admired, early baroque style of the Carracci.

West, who became "history painter" to George III, as well as his good friend, and followed Reynolds as President of the Royal Academy, painted his early history pieces in a style similar to that of this *Self Portrait*. Faces, hands, even figures were tightly modeled, and a warm, smoky ambience, recalling Lodovico Carracci's work, was frequently used. In this portrait the very free brushwork of the curtain and the "painterly" treatment of the sky, probably indicate that they were added later by West, who frequently retouched his pictures. At any rate, these details resemble the style West developed in the 1780's and 1790's.

West's late style is evident in *Belisarius and the Boy*, painted over thirty years later in 1802. In those years West had experienced amazing success and was unchallenged in the field of history painting. Perhaps, as a result, a certain carelessness developed in his style; at times he is perfunctory in the execution of specific forms. But West was not interested in the precise articulation of his figures; he was concerned with literary content. Further, he kept pace with the most progressive aesthetic thought of his age. After being a pioneer in neo-classicism, he moved on to anticipate many aspects of romantic art (Kimball, 1932, pp. 403-10). He was influenced by the theories of Edmund Burke and Richard Payne Knight. In *Belisarius*, West is illustrating Knight's idea that strongly expressed emotions are sublime. Justinian's greatest general is shown in his old age, and, as a blind and beggared outcast, he excites the commiseration of a youth who knew of his former conquests. Belisarius sits beneath an inscription attesting to his service in restoring the fortifications of the city, and below him is a fallen relief showing a commander crowned by Fame. West's interest was to stir the observer's emotions, to make him sympathetically experience the shock of the boy at the ingratitude of the Emperor who so neglected his faithful general. While this kind of painting is not popular today, it had great originality prior to the Victorian era.

Grose Evans

Nineteenth Century

Mary Cassatt
American, 1845-1926

49 WOMAN AND CHILD DRIVING 1879
Oil on canvas; 35 1/4 x 51 1/2 inches
Signed lower right: *Mary Cassatt*
Lent by the Commissioners of Fairmount Park
W. P. Wilstach Collection
Courtesy of the Philadelphia Museum of Art

In 1874 Mary Cassatt settled in Paris to pursue her art career after studying works by earlier European masters in Italy, Spain and the Netherlands and thus equipping herself with the necessary technical knowledge to succeed in having her paintings accepted in the Paris *Salons*. She soon realized, however, that her loyalties belonged with the modern, experimental artists — the impressionists. She was delighted therefore to accept Degas' invitation to join the group in 1877. The following years, during which her friendship with Degas grew, were among her most productive.

Woman and Child Driving shows Degas' strong influence. In it are pictured her sister, Lydia, who was her favorite model during those formative years, and little Odile Fèvre, who was Degas' niece. The main focus is on the two firmly modeled figures, treated with true understanding of their individual characteristics. The groom at the jump-seat serves as a splendid foil to the delicately featured, serious child and the strong, alert woman driving. He lends a humorous note to this vigorous work, executed with zestful courage. The liveliness of the composition is enhanced by the luminosity of the color scheme which is more impressionistic than in her late works. Her emphasis on academic draftsmanship then became more dominant and, under the influence of Japanese prints, the flattening of the design was of greater concern to her. In this early work the bold foreshortening and cropping of the pony and cart and the asymmetry of the composition are expressive of Mary Cassatt's independent viewpoint and youthful

50 AT THE DRESSING TABLE 1909
Oil on canvas; 36 1/2 x 28 1/2 inches
Signed lower right: *Mary Cassatt*
Lent from the Collection of Mrs. Samuel E. Johnson

prowess. These qualities enabled her to cope with Degas' difficult disposition and accept his criticism as well as his encouragement.

In the winter of 1897 she made her first trip home since settling in and near Paris. Over twenty years had passed, during which time she had gained the admiration and respect of her fellow artists and of many French critics. At this time she started to help Mr. and Mrs. H. O. Havemeyer in the formation of their great collection of old masters and impressionists and acted as well as art adviser to many other American friends. Consequently she became less absorbed in her own work. Her painting *At the Dressing Table* is distinguished by an interesting composition, definitely influenced by her study of Japanese prints. The use of the arabesque as well as the echoing circles of the mirror in its mahogany frame and the smaller round hand mirror point up this exotic element. The balancing of the warm and cool colors is handsomely contrived, and the brushwork is freely and surely applied to form this fine example from the culminating period of her career when she considered patterns and design of primary importance.

The choice of the intimate scene of the dressing room is characteristic of Cassatt's honest, forthright nature as was her dominant theme of "mother and child." She painted what she knew and thoroughly understood, an attitude reflecting her artistic integrity.

Adelyn D. Breeskin

Paul Cézanne
French, 1839-1906

At a time when the slogan of the realist school was that *il faut être de son temps,* Cézanne was turning back to the seventeenth century to "do Poussin over after nature." Though the return to the seventeenth century had been a source of inspiration for French artists from David to Manet, Cézanne seems to have been the only one to comprehend that century's concern with formal structure. In *Still Life with Bread and Eggs* another aspect of the art of that period appears: that of Dutch still life.

In the mid-1860's Cézanne shows the influence of the somber colors and rich paint surface of Courbet. An important aspect of the *Still Life with Bread and Eggs* is the tactile quality of its surface, which helps to relieve the austerity of its color. In addition, Cézanne shows his early preoccupation with the creation of an architecture of formal rela-

tionships between space and object. Though some of the relationships may seem crude and the background may appear lacking in vitality, the picture has the quality of excitement generated by a twenty-six year old artist groping toward a new art.

More than thirty years later Cézanne applied his developed ideas concerning the structure of painting to *Mont Sainte-Victoire Seen from Bibémus Quarry.* Studying the internal relationships of the landscape, he has selected for emphasis those elements that lend themselves to a clear expression of organic form. Like Poussin, Cézanne sought to avoid the unclear suggestion of infinity and has defined the picture within the space created between the inactive foreground and the limiting form of Mont Sainte-Victoire. Laterally the picture is terminated on the right by the large tree which is cut off

51 STILL LIFE WITH BREAD AND EGGS 1865
Oil on canvas; 23 1/4 x 30 inches
Signed and dated lower left:
P. Cezanne/ 1865
Lent by the Cincinnati Art Museum

at the edge of the canvas. In ordering the forms in his picture, the artist has chosen a distant though definable viewpoint so that the quarry and the mountain can be encompassed in an integrated space. Counterbalancing the effect of perspective resulting from a distant viewpoint, he has used color to emphasize the plasticity of forms.

Between the execution of *Still Life with Bread and Eggs* and *Mont Sainte-Victoire* he had discovered through impressionism the potential of color. While the impressionists were primarily concerned with the relation of color to color, Cézanne realized that the modulation of color could be used to express form.

Color has a special value, furnishing a means of expressing interrelationships of forms in space rather than fixing the absolute position of forms in space as occurs in perspective-projection. Through the use of color, Cézanne stresses his feeling for plasticity, while at the same time he preserves the effectiveness of the surface of the canvas as an aesthetic object. While impressionist works often retain only the shimmer of sensuously rich surfaces, Cézanne was able to combine this surface richness with a strong articulation of form. He had fulfilled his goal: "to make something solid of impressionism."

Christopher Gray

52   MONT SAINTE-VICTOIRE
SEEN FROM BIBEMUS QUARRY   c.1898-1900
Oil on canvas; 25 1/2 x 32 inches
The Baltimore Museum of Art
Cone Collection

Thomas Cole
American, 1801-48

53 LANDSCAPE:
SCENE FROM THE LAST OF THE MOHICANS 1827
Oil on canvas; 25 x 35 inches
Signed and dated lower center: *T. Cole/ 1827*
Lent by the New York State Historical Association

Landscape: Scene from The Last of the Mohicans is a splendid example of the paintings upon which Cole's early fame was based, deeply expressive of his feelings for the philosophic and religious values of the American wilderness and his belief in nature — as Alison put it, ". . . as the temple of the Living God, in which praise is due . . ." The immediate popularity of such works clearly attests to the ebullient nationalism of the time and the pride in, and early nostalgia for, the unspoiled land and its autumnal splendors. Like most of Cole's works, it is a composition, painted in the studio from various sketches made in the area of the White Mountains and around Lake George. The inclusion of an episode from Cooper's then latest novel, which enhances the "Americanism" of the work, had been suggested by Robert Gilmor, Jr. of Baltimore, who had commissioned the painting. Executed on a small scale and in a rather detailed fashion, this picture displays a technical mastery and accomplished handling of light, color and composition unmatched by any other American landscapist of the time. We are not dealing here with an ordinary "view taker" or topographer but with an artist of unusual sensitivity and imagination, eminently qualified to be the leader of our first native school of painting.

Seventeen years, of which more than four were spent abroad, separate this work from the *Mount Aetna from Taormina, Sicily*. Although Cole had continued to paint compositions of wild scenery, his interest had become focused on landscape of a more obvious allegorical, literary and moralizing sort. By 1844 he had succeeded in raising landscape to the level of history painting in the academic hierarchy of genres. He had painted *The Course of Empire, Voyage of Life, Il Penseroso* and *L'Allegro, Departure* and *Return, The Past* and *The Present,* and numerous single works like *Dream of Arcadia* wherein he, as Asher Durand said, demonstrated the high moral capabilities of landscape painting. It was by now Cole's firm belief that art should not merely please, but exalt, ennoble and instruct.

54 MOUNT AETNA FROM TAORMINA,
SICILY 1844
Oil on canvas; 32 1/2 x 48 inches
Signed and dated on column drum, lower center:
T. Cole/ 1844
Lent by the Lyman Allyn Museum

In February of 1844 he wrote to Daniel Wadsworth that he considered the painting of subjects of a moral and religious nature the great and serious mission of the artist, and that "work ought not to be a dead imitation of things without the power to impress a sentiment, or enforce a truth." Such are the thoughts underlying *Mount Aetna* which must have been associated in Cole's mind with *The Course of Empire*. This assumption is based on various statements of the artist. When *The Course of Empire* series could not be made available for his exhibition in December 1843, Cole wrote his wife that he had determined to make up for the series by painting as a substitute a large picture of Mount Aetna from Taormina (this was a slightly earlier version of the painting included in this exhibition). Even more meaningful are the references found in Cole's article on "Sicilian Scenery and Antiquities" (1844, p. 242). Describing the rise and fall of ancient civilizations in words that evoke his earlier pictorial descriptions of

their destiny in *The Course of Empire,* Cole perceives Mount Aetna as the symbol of permanence in contrast to man's transiency. The artist has succeeded in translating this conception into his painting of 1844 in which he contrasts the majestic mountain with the ruins of the Greek theater in Taormina.

In this context it should be noted that, unlike the early *Scene from the Last of the Mohicans* and the majority of his mature and late works, *Mount Aetna* is less a "composition-picture" than an accurate panoramic view, despite its profound associations. It is based on a detailed drawing, whose accuracy in both general effect and details can be confirmed by photographs of the scene. The larger scale and broader handling — that "free and robust boldness" noted by Bryant — reflect the change in Cole's style resulting from greatly expanded experience. But the artist as poet and philosopher has remained the same.

Howard S. Merritt

John Constable
British, 1776-1837

Constable's *Dedham Vale* is one of his earliest works to reveal the pursuit of goals that would preoccupy him for the rest of his life. Painted in September 1802, when he was still a student in the Royal Academy Schools, it shows him carrying out a resolution which he had expressed in a letter written the preceding May: "For these two past years I have been running after pictures and seeking the truth at second-hand. I have . . . endeavored to make my performances look as if really *executed* by other men . . . I shall shortly return to Bergholt where I shall make some laborious studies from nature — and I shall endeavor to get a pure and unaffected representation of the scenes that may employ me . . . " (Reynolds, 1960, pp. 45-46). The picture still reflects his dependence on other artists; its composition is based on Claude Lorrain's *Hagar and the Angel,* which was then in the collection of Constable's friend and patron Sir George Beaumont (now in the National Gallery, London) and of which Constable had made a copy two years before. Nonetheless, Constable's obvious struggle to make his picture "a pure and unaffected representation" of the Suffolk countryside marks the hesitant beginnings of what would remain the central goal of his artistic activity.

Constable's progress over the next twenty years was a slow step-by-step fulfillment of what he set out to do in 1802. Once achieved, however, in such monumental scenes of rural tranquility as *The White Horse* of 1819 (Frick Collection) or *The Hay Wain* of 1821 (National Gallery, London) his pure and unaffected representation began to give way to a more emotional vision of nature. By the end of the 1820's the prevailing character of his art was one of stormy agitation, and he was developing a conspicuous manner of covering his pictures with touches of white paint to provide flickering accents of light. Between the death of his wife in 1828 and the end of his own life in 1837, Constable generally seems to have been plunged into a deep gloom which is given full expression in his art.

The Dell in Helmingham Park of 1830 is one of various versions of a subject which began to occupy Constable in 1823; he had sketched in the park as early as 1800, so the picture is not an unalloyed product of his last years. It does, however, show his late manner of execution. Also, the sinuous forms of the trees, which blot out the sky, might be compared to the oppressively dramatic clouds which fill the heavens of other pictures of the late 1820's and the 1830's. Although the scene is far from stormy, the

55 DEDHAM VALE 1802
Oil on canvas; 17 1/8 x 13 1/2 inches
Dated and inscribed on stretcher:
Sep 1802 John [. . .] Isabel Constable
Lent by the Victoria and Albert Museum

56 THE DELL IN HELMINGHAM PARK 1830
Oil on canvas; 44 5/8 x 51 1/2 inches
Lent by the Nelson Gallery-Atkins Museum
Nelson Fund

nervous handling and the restricted point of view make the picture seem like a vision of an isolated and private place of escape rather than the open and sunlit world of rustic well-being depicted in the artist's works of a few years earlier.

Despite the changed mood of Constable's last years, his career shows a remarkable continuity. Many of his mature works are richer, more accomplished and more expressive reworkings of themes that occupied him in his student days. Thus, the small *Dedham Vale* of 1802 served as model for a large picture of the same subject (now in the National Gallery of Scotland) which Constable painted and exhibited in 1828.

Both the early and the late work exhibited here were painted in locations of close proximity to each other. *Dedham Vale* depicts a scene near the village of East Bergholt where Constable grew up, while *The Dell in Helmingham Park* shows a site only a few miles away which was the property of the Dysart family with whom the artist had lifelong connections. His deep and abiding affection for the landscape of his native Suffolk was one of the wellsprings of his art, and to its scenery he constantly returned for subjects, from the very beginning of his career to the very end.

Allen Staley

Jean-Baptiste-Camille Corot
French, 1796-1875

Corot's contemporaries were mainly familiar with two aspects of his art: the heroic, idealized landscapes, which are composites of studies made from nature, and the "invented" pictures of his later years, the nostalgic *souvenirs* and *reveries* that brought him fame and wealth. During his lifetime Corot saw to it that — with relatively few exceptions — the art world remained unaware of his plein-air studies and his figure pieces, the works on which his reputation rests today. Corot's own satisfaction with his accomplishments in these areas leaves only one explanation for his reluctance to share these works with the public at large — his compliance with what he considered the taste of his epoch.

An obedient son, Corot was twenty-six years old and without any training as a painter, when in 1822 he finally obtained his family's consent to pursue an artist's career. He sought instruction from Achille Michallon who was his own age, but their

relationship was cut short the same year by the latter's death. Nevertheless, a faithful Corot always named his friend as his first teacher, perhaps because it was Michallon who had impressed on him that working directly from nature was an absolute prerequisite for a landscape painter.

Corot adhered to this advice — never obtaining more enchanting results than the diminutive pictures of Rome and the Campagna he executed during his first stay in Italy from 1825-28. *Rome: Bridge and Castle of St. Angelo . . .* is one of the most successful examples of these years. Endowed with an extraordinary gift of observation and a special penchant for selecting his motifs, Corot painted several different views of this site which contained so many elements that fascinated him: the bridge which not only lends structure to the scene but also permits the painter to indicate the play of light that changes from arch to arch; the monumental circular form of the castle

57   ROME: BRIDGE AND CASTLE OF ST. ANGELO
WITH CUPOLA OF ST. PETER'S   1826-27
Oil on canvas; 8 5/8 x 15 inches
Stamp of Vente Corot lower left
Lent by the California Palace
of the Legion of Honor
Collis Potter Huntington Memorial Collection

58 THE CROWN OF FLOWERS 1865-70
Oil on canvas; 25 1/2 x 17 inches
Signed lower right: *COROT*
The Abram Eisenberg Collection
On Indefinite Loan to
The Baltimore Museum of Art

counterpoised by the rectangular buildings on the opposite side of the Tiber; and rising in the background, Michelangelo's spectacular dome balanced and integrated in the composition by the large triangular-shaped reflection in the water. As firmly constructed as the architecture it depicts, this painting, like most of Corot's early Italian sketches, is distinguished by its sparkling luminosity, variety of textures and tonal harmonies — qualities that express the young artist's consummate skill and serene temperament.

Most of the fundamental elements of his early style can be found in his late works, though they may not be conspicuous in pictures of his invention — those all too numerous silvery glades with dancing nymphs and arcadic shepherds which now have fallen from public favor. However, in the best of these nostalgic *souvenirs* the superb control of color harmonies, the astute rendering of dawn or dusk and the ease of composition and execution attest to Corot's rare artistic talents.

There is no question that Corot's figure pieces created during the last fifteen years of his life are today the most cherished works of his late style. In this writer's opinion *The Crown of Flowers* is among the most poetic and pictorially most beautiful of this group. These figures of women constitute the full realization of his genius — the results of his unequalled sense of observation successfully paired with imagination. Working from the model (dressed in clothes obtained from a theatrical firm) Corot in *The Crown of Flowers* has invented the surroundings intended only as a foil for the seated girl. The figure itself shares the solid structural form, the rich impasto, the exquisite tonal values and the sensuous textures with his early Roman landscapes. But now a mood of gentle melancholy prevails. As Alfred Barr has pointed out, these women are steeped in reverie and neglect their tasks — they do not fill their water jugs or play their lutes or ever finish the wreath of flowers in their hands. Thus, Barr (1930, p. 16) has asked: "What caused Corot, the robust Vergilian, to fall under this pall of neoplatonic lassitude? Was he in his old age visited by the spirit of Giorgione who died so young?"

G. R.

Hilaire Germain Edgar Degas
French, 1834-1917

The artistic personality of Hilaire Germain Edgar Degas is full of irony and paradox. Georges Rivière described him as *un bourgeois de Paris.* If the bourgeois is conservative and traditionalist, Degas in many ways was artistically as well as personally bourgeois. His style emerged out of that peculiar combination of classicism, romanticism and realism that was called *le juste milieu* and constituted the fundamental aesthetic for much of academic painting down to the twentieth century — an aesthetic which to a considerable extent is illustrated in the work of Ingres, whom Degas so much admired. More than most of his avant-garde associates, he studied the art of the past and as late as 1870 copied a Poussin in the Louvre. Even his alliance with the impressionists was in large part a convenience. The formless flux of color and light did not hold the same fascination for him that it did for the others; throughout his career he was intent on structuring space, and his impressionism, if it can be called that, was of attitude and gesture, station point and angle of vision.

Yet as we study the man and his work, more and more he seems tentatively to be investigating possibilities that will become commonplace in the twentieth century. From the very beginning he interprets humanity with a new psychological perception grounded in reality rather than in literature and earlier art. And in his interest in photography, in his attempt not simply to record gestures and attitudes but to develop sequential movements of shape across the canvas, in his involvement with abstract pattern and in his exploration of the potentialities of mixed media, he anticipates many of the preoccupations of his successors. In fact, his increasing tendency to limit his work to the theme of the dancer and bather suggests a desire more characteristic of the twentieth century than his own — to create a vocabulary of forms he could arrange as he saw fit in a setting of his own creation and to find a style in which matter is less important than manner. The two pictures exhibited suggest the polarities of his development, in which portrait becomes genre and genre becomes abstraction.

The *Portrait of René de Gas,* his younger brother, associates itself with the style of Ingres in its precise definition of form, carefully modeled volumes, knife-edged descriptive brushwork and Raphaelesque shapes and proportions. Already, however, even in this relatively formal scheme, there is a sense of the transitory moment and the incipient movement that adumbrates his

59 PORTRAIT OF RENE DE GAS c.1855
Oil on canvas; 36 1/4 x 29 1/2 inches
Lent by the Smith College Museum of Art

60　PORTRAIT OF ROSE CARON　c.1890
Oil on canvas; 30 x 32 1/2 inches
Stamp of Vente Degas lower left
Lent by the Albright-Knox Art Gallery

later interest in portraying his sitters in action.

The *Portrait of Rose Caron* is a superb example of his late style. Though it was painted around 1890, some eighteen years before the last entry in Lemoisne's catalogue, it is nevertheless one of the last paintings in oil; for after that date Degas turned more and more exclusively to pastel and, his eyesight failing, completed relatively few works. The sitter was a soprano whom Degas admired as much for her controlled gesture as for her voice. And, as if still pursuing a project he had outlined in his journals as a youth — to study hands in all their casual and ritualistic movements — he concentrates not on her head but her gesture, showing how she pulls on her gloves with a deft, decisive and gracefully elegant movement that gains significance from its isolation against the contrasting tone of the background.

By this time the recorded gesture is a relatively conservative aspect of his work. More significant and provocative are the formal qualities of the composition: the peculiar character of the shapes, which send elongated extensions into the surrounding space; the harmony established between positive and negative shapes; the movement of forms across the canvas, with the body, the chair and the contours of the shawl repeating in variation the rhythm of the arms; the studied imbalance of masses and tones; the sumptuous variety of the painted surface; and the implications of spontaneity and directness in the touch, which weaves the contrasting elements together; the concern, in short, for formal values. Despite all that intervenes, the distance between the painting of Rose Caron and paintings of the 1950's seems astonishingly short.

Lincoln Johnson

Ferdinand Victor Eugène Delacroix
French, 1798-1863

No other painter is more popularly identified with nineteenth-century romanticism than Eugène Delacroix. His reputation as a rebel, however, he neither desired nor wholly deserved. In fact, Delacroix was as much an exceptional, isolated figure within his age as a sovereign representative of it. Throughout his life he remained curiously alienated from the present. He dwelt more in the past and the future. He himself sensed something of that uneasy ambivalence. As an older man, grateful for Baudelaire's unqualified praise of his work, he gently chided the young poet for treating him as already "one of the great dead." Few of Delacroix's contemporaries were prepared to understand — far less, to accept — the inherent tensions of his creative situation. His youthful devotion to sensuous and dramatic effects had appeared to represent open defiance of prevailing aesthetic values. His fundamental belief in tradition was obscured by an individualism so pronounced as to seem "eccentric." But Delacroix's capacity to use convention as the vehicle of personal expression grew with the years. Indeed, it may now be regarded as his special gift. His borrowings from earlier art have the air of originality and his innovations, the stamp of historical authority. The two paintings by Delacroix in the present exhibition illustrate aspects of that broad course of his artistic development.

The *Battle of Poitiers* is a study for a much larger canvas commissioned by the Duchess of Berry. The Duchess' flight from France at the time of the Revolution of 1830 prevented delivery of the work to her, but nevertheless a partial payment was made. Ironically, those proceeds helped finance Delacroix's painting of *Liberty Leading the People,* in which the civil uprising that had occasioned his patroness' exile was celebrated. As is often the case with the smaller, more personal works by Delacroix, the oil sketch of the *Battle of Poitiers* reveals his traits of style and concept with particular clarity. The scene is one of impending military disaster. King John III of France and his young son are shown in the ebb of a futile struggle against the forces of Edward, the Black Prince. The very massing of the composition announces the outcome of the battle, as the last pockets of French resistance are about to be overwhelmed by English might. Those knots of

61 SKETCH FOR
'THE BATTLE OF POITIERS' 1829-30
Oil on canvas; 20 3/4 x 25 1/2 inches
Initialed lower right: *E D*
Lent by The Walters Art Gallery

vivid, colorful action lend dramatic moment as well as formal focus to the swirl of interlocking figures. And the suggestive, open handling of the paint intensifies the overall impact of pulsing agitation. In granting full prominence to the direct, sensory appeals of color and shape in his call upon the viewer's imaginative response, Delacroix has raised the familiar, historical genre of battle painting from the status of narrative episode to that of visual event. If he has somewhat tempered the "excesses" of personal mannerism, which had been imputed to his *Death of Sardanapalus,* he has sacrificed none of the richness of color and animation of surface that had from the beginning been the hallmark of his art.

Christ on the Sea of Galilee represents a later phase of Delacroix's development. Roughly a quarter century of intervening experience had modified, if not diverted, his aims. His trip to Morocco in 1832 had left indelible impressions of an exotic reality in which new possibilities of coloristic expression were revealed. His subsequent engagement as a muralist, on the other hand, had confronted him with the practical need of adopting more systematic procedures than he had previously employed. Speculative by temperament, he sought theoretical guidance both in the study of natural effects and in the example of the baroque and Venetian masters he always had admired.

The remarkable freshness of touch in the *Christ on the Sea of Galilee* hardly disguises the extent to which youthful spontaneity has been absorbed in the mature search for synthesis. A more reasoned order of color has been devised to project an encompassing world of light and atmosphere; and the central drama is integral with the universal state of the surrounding elements. As in Delacroix's other, closely related versions of the subject, Christ's miraculous calm at the eye of nature's threatening turbulence recalls the painter's faith in the powers of Mind. His will to unite reason with sensibility had informed his effort to create forms that were at once true to his personal vision and fit to the measure of the old masters, whom he regarded as his only real rivals.

Frank Andersen Trapp

62   CHRIST ON THE SEA OF GALILEE   1854
Oil on canvas; 23 1/2 x 28 7/8 inches
Signed and dated lower right:
Eug. Delacroix, 1854
Lent by The Walters Art Gallery

Thomas Eakins
American, 1844-1916

In 1870 Thomas Eakins returned from four years of study abroad to his father's house in Philadelphia, never to leave the United States again. He seems to have been unaware of the impressionists while he was a student, and yet Eakins and the impressionists recorded life around them with similar partisanship. Aesthetics aside, both re-examined and transformed sentimental genre into a vigorous record of their time and place. The introduction of urban subjects by the impressionists may have been as revolutionary as their aesthetic innovations. The pictures of Manet, Monet, Renoir and Degas are windows onto a spectacle of bourgeois pleasures painted so sensuously and affectionately, we have all become impressionist voyeurs peeping nostalgically into an enchanted past.

But if the carefree approach was possible in Paris, it was certainly a different world to which Eakins had returned, a society involved in serious business, advancing in science and industry, creating material wealth. If Eakins comprehended the new spirit reshaping the country, he must have viewed it optimistically, since he shared its admiration for machinery, science and technology. It is possible he felt that this concord would make him an acceptable interpreter of the new social structure and help his career. His purpose was to reconcile creation with observation, to interpret nature through intellectual and scientific scrutiny.

Shortly after his return, Eakins painted *Home Scene*. His joy at being reunited with his family must have been intense. The painting shows Eakins' sisters, Margaret and Caroline, in their Philadelphia home. Margaret, at the piano, caught in a mood of deep reverie, is looking down at the younger Caroline, only abstractedly conscious of the child's presence. Both figures are isolated in that stillness which foreshadows the lonely quality in most of Eakins' works, whether it is a man in a boat or a surgeon in an operating amphitheater. A cat, barely perceptible, adds the domestic touch in quite a different spirit from the feline in Manet's *Olympia,* though it is amusing to conjecture that Eakins might have seen the famous painting. Eakins' aesthetic weapon is chiaroscuro, and his masterly use of it enables him to make the forms large, simple and strong.

Genre painting, with its characteristic insistence on minutiae and meticulous handling did not interest Eakins. He exaggerated and distorted in his struggle to bring ex-

pressive qualities to the subject. What academician would have allowed himself the liberty of rendering Margaret's right hand so awkwardly? But what a beautiful transition it makes from the darker portion of the figure to the head, catching the light that is fully revealed on the face. The triangle created by Margaret's right arm is repeated within the space enclosed by her

63 HOME SCENE 1870-71
Oil on canvas; 21 3/4 x 18 inches
Signed lower right and on back: *Eakins*
Lent by The Brooklyn Museum

84

64 PORTRAIT OF MRS. EDITH MAHON 1904
Oil on canvas; 20 x 16 inches
Inscribed, signed and dated on back:
TO MY FRIEND EDITH MAHON,
THOMAS EAKINS, 1904
Lent by the Smith College Museum of Art

arm resting on the piano. In fact, the entire composition is triangular, a device he learned from studying the old masters. But the painting is also marked by an unusual freedom in handling. The touches of clear blue in the child's dress, the repetition of red in both figures and the deliberate placing of an orange on the piano, attest to Eakins' awareness as a colorist. Even the complex patterns of the rug are suggested by dabs of pure color. This self-assurance is indicated also by the manner in which the details of the piano are sketched in, implying rather than modeling the form. The quality of reality which is inherent in this and future works is achieved without the rhetoric or sentimentality that would have assured his success, had his vision been less profound.

Toward the latter part of his life, having suffered from the indifference displayed toward his most ambitious works, Eakins became primarily a painter of portraits. Commissions were few, but portraiture permitted him to continue working from nature, while it offered him contact with people who interested him. Among those who sat for him were fellow painters, musicians, clerics, professors, scientists — people with whom Eakins could communicate, and even some who were willing to sit for an artist about whom the uneasy feeling persisted that he might have greatness after all.

Mrs. Edith Mahon was a professional singer. Eakins' perception of human character is especially eloquent in her portrait. The face is modeled in half shadow with the strong light on the neck and chest directing our eye to return to the face, as one returns to a shadowed room after too much sunlight. This is a modern face, distinguished and solidly structured. Tragic, self-absorbed and resigned, this woman seems enchanted, fascinated by some inner revelation.

Portrait of Mrs. Edith Mahon was painted twelve years before the artist's death. It reveals a power and insight which distinguish Eakins from the other painters of his generation, none of whom felt so deeply, saw so clearly, took such delight in observed fact or painted it with such integrity. He is the last great American master of the renaissance tradition. His paintings were too revealing, too unflattering for his contemporaries. Eakins flouted no aesthetic conventions, introduced no novelties or reforms, but his insistence on searching for the truth was too much for a society unwilling to see itself as it was.

Abram Lerner

Paul Gauguin
French, 1848-1903

Paul Gauguin started painting in the early seventies. Joining the group of the impressionists, he became especially influenced by Pissarro and in 1883 decided to make painting his career. A year later he was desperate for money and moved from Paris to Rouen, hoping that living there would be cheaper and sales better.

In 1884 the impressionist movement was beginning to break apart. Cézanne was developing his ideas concerning the expression of form through color, Durand-Ruel called the works executed by Monet that year *fauve,* while Pissarro was about to take up the neo-impressionist theories of Seurat and Signac. Renoir had gone back to classical art for inspiration. Gauguin, too, shows the beginnings of his future tendencies, in a tentative way, in his painting of the *Church of St. Ouen* in Rouen. Superficially the picture still maintains the fragmented brush stroke similar to that Pissarro used in the early eighties, but the color is no longer impressionist. The palette is dark and rich. There is little differentiation within objects of light and shadow, and often the most intense colors sparkle like jewels against the dark green velvet of the foliage. Gauguin was not yet using the massive areas of color that he was to employ

65 CHURCH OF ST. OUEN, ROUEN 1884
Oil on canvas; 36 1/8 x 28 1/2 inches
Signed and dated lower right: *P. Gauguin 84*
Lent by Wildenstein and Co., Inc.

in a few years in the pictures he would paint in Brittany and Tahiti, but he was already thinking in terms of sumptuous color rather than effects of light.

While the *Church of St. Ouen* was painted only one year after Gauguin decided to become a professional artist, *Sister of Charity* was painted only a year before his death. In spite of the shell of brilliant color, it is a somber picture. Ever since 1887, and his near suicide, Gauguin had been preoccupied with the meaning of life. In 1901 he had left Tahiti to seek his last Eden in the Marquesas, but he found a sad group of islands, peopled by a dying race that no longer had a will to live. Here, face to face with a spiritual despair as great as his own, Gauguin for the first time saw the Polynesian, not as some joyous, carefree inhabitant of a paradise, but rather as a human being with a soul capable of suffering.

While the early picture by Gauguin is full of vitality and sensuous richness, this picture, at the end of his life, is austere. The paint is thin and the brush stroke is calm and measured in its rhythms. Yet two figures stand out. One is the nun on the left, whose blue robe and composed posture recall the garb and pose of the Breton woman at the foot of the wayside Calvary in Gauguin's *Yellow Christ,* painted thirteen years earlier. The other figure is that of the standing Polynesian in yellow. Perhaps again, blue is the color symbolic of the purity of the Virgin, and yellow the color of degradation and misery. For while Gauguin in his early *Church of St. Ouen* had been preoccupied with the outward appearance of things, in his later works he was concerned with creating symbols for their inner meaning.

Christopher Gray

66 SISTER OF CHARITY 1902
Oil on canvas; 25 5/8 x 29 7/8 inches
Signed and dated lower left:
Paul Gauguin 1902
Lent by the Marion Koogler McNay Art Institute

Vincent van Gogh
Dutch, 1853-90

67 LABORER'S COTTAGE AT NUENEN   1885
Oil on canvas; 25 1/4 x 30 3/4 inches
Signed lower left: *Vincent*
Lent by the Stedelijk Museum
Vincent van Gogh Foundation

Vincent van Gogh's life as an artist was limited to nine years during which he produced six hundred paintings and over eight hundred water colors and drawings. Although in the brief period of his artistic activity his means of expression underwent many obvious and definable changes, Vincent's concept of his mission as a painter and his artistic aims remained consistent and were revealed in his earliest works.

At first glance *Laborer's Cottage at Nuenen,* painted at a time of great personal unhappiness, may seem to be just another realistic landscape by a Dutch follower of the Barbizon School. The subject matter is ordinary enough — depicted over and over again since the seventeenth century, when Dutch artists first dared to use such a simple motif as the sole content of a painting.

However, the thoughtful observer will notice that Vincent's treatment of this subject evokes an emotional response usually associated with the works of his artistic maturity. The somber color is not relieved but intensified by the orange and sulphur-yellow streaks in the sky, just as the graceful lines of the two trees at right do not relieve but emphasize the oppressive shape of the cottage.

In its use of color and line and the expressiveness of the brush stroke, *Laborer's Cottage* supersedes naturalistic description and conveys the artist's subjective feeling. Thus, this early work anticipates Vincent's later unique achievement: to record reality — whether people, still lifes or landscapes — together with his own emotional reaction to his subject. That this was already his goal at the time of the Nuenen picture is stated in a letter he wrote in 1884 or 1885 to his brother Theo: ". . . my great ambition is to achieve those inaccuracies, deviations, deformations and changes of reality that may well be lies, if one wishes, but are truer than literal truth" (1958, II, p. 397, #418).

The final fulfillment of Vincent's ambition can be observed in *Stairway at Auvers* painted one month before his self-inflicted death. The following comments are excerpts from Professor Meyer Schapiro's brilliant discussion of the painting in his monograph *Van Gogh* (1950, p. 126): ". . . A scene of many convergences and encounters, focused upon a central region at the foot of the steps, it has no real dominant; the general effect is governed by the hectic movement of unsteady diagonal lines imposed upon objects of unlike character. The repetition of this restless theme is so impulsive, however, and contains so many interesting variations that the painting . . . becomes a work of intense passion and concentrated seeing. We discover contrasting straight lines in the buildings, stabilizing horizontals and verticals, the important red roofs, and numerous touches like the yellow hats, the yellow doorway and the dark windows (which recall the women's skirts) — deliberate oppositions to the prevailing instability, yet not altogether opposed to it in their own spottedness. Here as in earlier paintings van Gogh practices that exchange of tones between far separated parts of the space (and between neighboring objects in different planes) which is one of his most effective unifying means. The same white tones with notes of blue and green occur in the distant house, in the dresses of the two girls in the foreground, and in the road and wall which they connect. In all this excitement of lines and spots there is also a note of buoyant gaiety and delight."

G. R.

68 STAIRWAY AT AUVERS 1890
Oil on canvas; 20 x 28 inches
Lent by the City Art Museum of St. Louis

Winslow Homer
American, 1836-1910

Winslow Homer's early work grew out of the nineteenth-century American genre tradition, with its devotion to country life and the world of childhood. He represented children with complete sympathy but with no trace of the mawkish sentimentality of the period. His boyhood idylls had the utter authenticity of Mark Twain's. Homer himself had continued into adult life his youthful enjoyment of outdoor activities, and his art pictured the world as a boy saw and felt it — but painted with a man's grasp of realities.

From the first, Homer's style was based on unusually direct observation of nature. As a young man he had said, "If a man wants to be an artist he should never look at pictures." Though this should be taken with a grain of salt, it is true that his early paintings, such as *Snap the Whip,* reveal little external influence. They were the works of a man who had looked much at nature but little at the art of others; they

had that rare and engaging quality — an innocent eye. In time his early naivete was to disappear, but he always retained his freshness of vision.

When Homer was in his late forties, fundamental changes took place in his life and work. Leaving New York, he settled on a lonely point of land on the Maine coast, Prout's Neck. Here his art reached full maturity. The idyllic world of country childhood disappeared. His dominant theme became the sea: its moods of storm and peace, its changing lights and colors, its unceasing movement. His later marines were among the most eloquent expressions in American art of the majesty and beauty of the ocean. Their nearest counterparts were Courbet's marines, more traditionally romantic, whereas Homer's were realistic, directly observed, vivid in their physical impact.

The direct relation to visual reality, that had marked him from the first, continued throughout his life. *West Point, Prout's Neck*

69 SNAP THE WHIP 1872
Oil on canvas; 22 x 36 1/2 inches
Signed and dated lower right: *HOMER 1872*
Lent by The Butler Institute of American Art

70 WEST POINT, PROUT'S NECK 1900
Oil on canvas; 30 1/4 x 48 1/4 inches
Signed and dated lower right: *Homer 1900*
Lent by the
Sterling and Francine Clark Art Institute

pictures the sea at flood tide just after the sun has set; the sky above the horizon is a crimson band, but the water, reflecting the light upper sky, is luminous and has a greenish and flesh-colored tonality against which the upflung spray shows dark and cold. Explaining "the peculiarity of light," Homer wrote: "The picture is painted *fifteen minutes* after sunset — not one minute before. . . . The light is from the sky in this picture. You can see it took many days of careful observation to get this (with a high sea & tide just right)." This was impressionism, but with a difference. Monet said that he was painting not objects but the color of the air between himself and them; but Homer's primary interest remained the thing-in-itself. He saw nature not as a purely visual phenomenon, but as a drama of elemental forces. His vision remained clear and exact, his style basically descriptive. The flowing movement of waves and leaping spray, and above all, the rhythmic design which captured the inexhaustible energy and freshness of the sea were as essential as the particular hour, light and color.

Lloyd Goodrich

Jean Auguste Dominique Ingres
French, 1780-1867

Although Ingres executed the Walters *Oedipus and the Sphinx* fifty years after his completion of the *Cardinal Bibiena* . . ., both these paintings were conceived during the same period, the years of his first stay in Rome; both are typical of his practice of duplicating and reworking themes and compositions that originated during the years 1806-1820 (Mongan, 1967, p. xx).

The earliest and largest (life size) of the three canvases of *Oedipus and the Sphinx* (Louvre) was painted in 1808, when Ingres was twenty-eight, as a student's *pièce réglementaire* at the French Academy in Rome. The London National Gallery owns a miniature *répétition* presumably dating from 1828. The version from the Walters Art Gallery was completed when Ingres was eighty-four, three years before his death. The figure of Oedipus, which is based directly on classical precedent, faces left in

the two earlier versions and right in the Walters example, and variations in detail help to relieve the later versions from being mere replicas of the first. In style, however, no change whatever has taken place between the first version and the last, although they are separated by a span of fifty-six years.

Cardinal Bibiena Presenting His Niece to Raphael, painted on the commission of Caroline Murat, Queen of Naples, presents a similar situation. This composition follows, with a few variations, a finished drawing of the scene, signed and dated 1812 (Louvre); it is repeated, again with a few variations, in another finished drawing of 1864 in the Fogg Art Museum (Mongan, 1967, No. 115).

The two paintings and their related works exemplify clearly enough the fusion of the two principal elements of Ingres' style: a certain "abstract" effect resulting from his

71 CARDINAL BIBIENA PRESENTING
HIS NIECE TO RAPHAEL c.1812
Oil on paper, mounted on fabric
23 1/4 x 18 1/4 inches
Signed lower left: *INGRES*
Lent by The Walters Art Gallery

early inclination as a *primitif* for flatness and unaccented contour lines, deriving especially from "Etruscan" (i.e. Greek) vase painting and encouraged by Flaxman's outline illustrations of Homer; and the greater depth, fullness of form, sensitivity and subtlety of contour modulations inspired by Raphael, whose *Madonna of the Chair* Ingres had copied at the age of twelve (Lapauze, 1910, p. 48).

As with Ingres' style, so with his character. His long career is famous for the essential consistency and changelessness of attitude manifested from start to finish. Ingres remained the same, even if the world did not. This continuity of outlook has been made the more familiar through the frequently quoted comments of his lifelong friend, M. E. J. Delécluze (1855, pp. 84-85): ". . . Ingres has not changed in looks or manner since his adolescence. . . The Ingres of 1854 has remained the same as the Ingres of 1797. . . All the characteristics that today are typical of this artist's talent — the finesse of contour, the true and profound feeling for form and the extraordinarily correct and firm modeling — all these qualities are already noticeable in his first attempts." Among major artists there can hardly be a more marked instance than that of Ingres where the ideas that control mature life appeared with such singular clarity at so early an age.

Edward S. King

72   OEDIPUS AND THE SPHINX   1864
Oil on canvas; 41 1/2 x 34 1/4 inches
Signed, inscribed and dated lower center:
J. Ingres pbat/ etatis/ LXXXIII/ 1864
Lent by The Walters Art Gallery

George Inness
American, 1825-94

73 THE SUN SHOWER 1847
Oil on canvas; 30 1/4 x 42 1/4 inches
Signed and dated lower center: *G. Inness 1847*
Lent by the Santa Barbara Museum of Art
Preston Morton Collection

The dramatic difference between the early and late examples of Inness' work reflects a corresponding evolution of attitude toward his subject, nature, as well as the general trend in American painting during this period. In its descriptive realism *The Sun Shower,* which predates the artist's first trip to Europe, suggests the pantheism that motivated his contemporaries of the Hudson River School. The spiritual significance of nature was to be indicated by means of minimal distortion of reality. Thus, the early view has the quality of being a portrait of a specific place, although it already contains certain personal elements of style that anticipate the artist's later developments. While his interest in light was characteristic of his whole generation, the luminous storm in the distance reveals Inness' special concern with haze and surprising light effects. Human activity in the landscape, including shepherdess and farmhands, emphasizes his preference, voiced much later, for "civilized" as opposed to "savage and untamed" landscape (*Harper's,* LVI, 1878, p. 461). Noteworthy is the preoccupation at this early date with compositional adjustments, particularly in the tonal cohesion of the shape of the dominant tree, whose right edge intersects the edge of the distant hill at right angles.

Near the Village, October reveals the culmination of several early tendencies. The now totally controlled rectilinear structure of interlocking tree trunks and horizon line expresses a mood of profound serenity. Unexpected lights flicker in the sky, in the grass, on a tree trunk, on distant buildings —

74 NEAR THE VILLAGE, OCTOBER 1892
Oil on canvas; 30 x 45 inches
Signed and dated lower left: *G. Inness 1892*
Lent by the Cincinnati Art Museum

lights that seem to emanate from the objects themselves (as do the colors) rather than from an identifiable natural source of illumination. The painted reality of the surface is no longer disguised. The shape-consciousness once limited to isolated elements of the view now controls the entire composition — a quality in keeping with the general trend of late nineteenth-century painting. A lone figure merges with the "civilized" field. The portrait character of the early view has been replaced by a generalized, simplified mental image. Such developments express a redirection of the artist's spiritual understanding of his subject. Now a follower of the more mystical pantheism of Emanuel Swedenborg, Inness rejected his earlier descriptive approach as "external" and preferred "those works of inspiration which allure the mind to the regions of the unknown" (*Harper's,* LVI, 1878, p. 461). All seems veiled in haze, suggesting, as Inness said, "a subtle essence . . . constituting an atmosphere about the bald detail of facts" (*Art Journal,* V, 1879, p. 376). Disparate details are obscured in "the great spiritual principle of unity" (*Harper's,* 1878, LVI, p. 461). Tangibility is sacrificed to dematerialization suggestive of flux. Similarities between Inness' late painted images and visionary landscape descriptions in Swedenborg's writings have been noted (Cikovsky, 1966, p. 6). Inness himself summarized the Swedenborgian assumptions underlying his late work: "Art is a subtle essence. It is not a thing of surfaces, but a moving spirit..." (*Art Journal,* V, 1879, p. 377).

Ila Weiss

Edouard Manet
French, 1832-83

Of the two paintings chosen as examples of Manet's early and late styles, *The Reader* illustrates one of a number of traditional genre subjects which appeared frequently in Manet's work of the 1860's. Such subjects involved a single figure shown frontally, in full or half length, in a still pose, centered on the canvas and in picturesque juxtaposition with still life objects. This genre, favored by many *Salon* exhibitors at the time, offered to the artist the advantage of relatively neutral, undramatic themes, and thus the opportunity of resolving primarily technical problems. Furthermore, with the presentation of one or, at most, two large forms (the figure and the book in *The*

75   THE READER   c.1861
Oil on canvas; 38 1/2 x 31 1/2 inches
Signed lower left: *Ed. Manet*
Lent by the City Art Museum of St. Louis

76 AT THE CAFE 1878
Oil on canvas; 18 5/8 x 15 3/8 inches
Signed lower left: *Manet*
Lent by The Walters Art Gallery

Reader) the difficulties of composition could be kept to a minimum. Manet seems to have been fully aware of these advantages, returning from time to time throughout his career to this basic format and subject category, revitalizing and renewing its conventions in the process.

At the Café represents a complete renewal within the genre category both in subject and in form. Its originality can best be measured by referring first to those permanent characteristics which it shares with *The Reader,* and which illustrate the "constants" of Manet's vision. The figures are shown in restful and natural postures which determine their gestures. Each, immersed in his own daydream, has a fixed, detached and slightly melancholy stare. In both compositions the identity and independence of each shape are preserved — be it a shirt front, a collar, a top hat, a hand or a vest button.

Within this stylistic framework, common to both paintings, the evolution of Manet's vision is clearly apparent. The more obvious symptoms of change in *At the Café* are the heightened color and the freer brushwork. The stable elements of the earlier composition (pyramidal figure; vertical plane and horizontal edge of the table; repeated triangular configurations; simple planear recession) have for the most part been replaced by a dynamic order of sharply contrasting and overlapping shapes. The entire surface is now energized. The tension established between the pattern of the picture plane and the structure in depth is intensified and vastly more complex. Figures and inanimate objects, solid forms and their intervals, are all given an equally positive pictorial role. Along the major diagonal of the composition three figures, shown in diminishing scale, are established within a wedge shape. The direction of their glances and the turn of their bodies are contrived so as to suggest abstractly, like the spokes of a wheel, a circular and fanning movement in depth.

The modernity of this painting, in contrast with the traditional character of *The Reader,* is not primarily expressed in the subject but in the new principle of relativity which determines its design and in the simultaneous impressions of order and flux conveyed by its composition. *At the Café* reveals Manet's discovery of a pictorial order which symbolizes the essence of modern mobility and impermanence.

Alain de Leiris

Claude Monet
French, 1840-1926

Of all the artists involved in the development of impressionism, only Claude Monet remained from beginning to end faithful to the conceptions and inherent qualities of this style. Shortly before his death in 1926 he restated that his only merit lay in painting "directly from nature, striving to render my impressions in the face of the most fugitive effects" (Seitz, 1960, p. 44). Both the early *Garden of the Princess, Louvre* and the late *Water Lilies* exhibit Monet's lifelong desire to translate into painterly equivalents his immediate perceptions of an ever-changing scene.

Monet's artistic purposes and goals, however, are only tentatively formulated and achieved in his early works of the 1860's. Although at this time he was in his own words "experimenting with light and color" (Rewald, 1961, p. 150) he was also practicing with more conventional subject matter and compositional formulas already refined by other nineteenth-century landscape painters such as Boudin, Corot and Courbet.

The highly structured, deep spatial composition of the *Garden of the Princess* gives the scene a sense of solidity and permanence which contrasts sharply with the active street passages where the shimmering, summarized forms threaten to rearrange themselves before our eyes. The landscape is symmetrically divided on either side of a vertical line descending from the Pantheon dome which dominates the skyline, but this stability of composition is broken in the lower section of the canvas. The rectangular garden is cut off in such a way as to form an awkward geometrical shape to the right of the central vertical line. This shape in turn conflicts with the balanced triangle formed by the garden to the left of the line. Perhaps this method of cutting off edges at odd angles was suggested by Japanese prints, fast gaining popularity in France at that time. Whatever its inspiration, the composition of this portion of the picture is decidedly unconventional and in conflict with the spatial structure employed throughout the rest of the painting. Interestingly enough, the garden itself is more conventionally handled in terms of light, color and brush stroke than any other part of the picture; it appears rather static, especially if compared with the sky and street areas where the sensation of moving light invigorates the forms.

In 1891 Monet created a magnificent water garden on his property in Giverny which in the late years of his life became his primary subject for contemplation and creation. He became more deeply absorbed

77 GARDEN OF THE PRINCESS, LOUVRE   c.1867
Oil on canvas; 36 1/8 x 24 3/8 inches
Signed lower right: *Claude Monet*
Lent by the Allen Memorial Art Museum
Oberlin College

and moved by the gentle daily occurrences of the lily pads and the shifting reflections on water than he had been by the constant transformation of the cityscape which lay before him in Paris. Oriented and committed as he was to the struggle of the artist's eye, mind and hand with the fleeting image, it was natural that he should have been attracted throughout his career to painting reflections. With the slightest movement of water causing a reshuffling of visual images and relationships, the continuous breakdown of perceived reality into abstract elements provided him with a constant challenge.

William Seitz (1960, p. 150) asks the question, "who before Monet would have dared to paint so insubstantial a motif" which would have served another painter only as background material. Monet's daring concentration on a limited yet endlessly changing world was coupled with innovating compositional devices. In *Water Lilies* all that happens above the water and all that exists on and below its surface is expressed by closely integrated planes of subtle horizontal and vertical progressions of color and form. No longer is there concern with ren-

dering deep space and solid shapes.

As with the early *Garden of the Princess*, the cutting off of the lily pads along the right side of the painting implies a continuation of the scene beyond the canvas, but here there is no conflict with the loosely structured, floating composition. The formal invention and the fluid handling of the brush and the color nuances which unify the disparate elements into a total visual experience are the accomplishments of a lifetime of intense dedication to the expression of natural and evanescent beauty.

Diana F. Johnson

78   WATER LILIES   c.1914
Oil on canvas; 63 1/4 x 71 1/8 inches
Signed lower right: *Claude Monet*
Lent by the Portland Art Museum

Camille Pissarro
French, 1830-1903

During the Franco-Prussian War of 1870-71 German troops were billeted in Pissarro's studio at Louveciennes, and most of his early output covering the period from 1855 to 1870 was either lost or damaged beyond repair. Among the works saved was *Path by the River,* an early masterpiece that as part of the George A. Lucas bequest to The Maryland Institute in 1910 came to Baltimore where for several decades it received scant notice.

Path by the River has been identified as a scene at La Varenne-Saint-Hilaire where Pissarro lived from 1863 to 1867. There, during his first extended stay in the French countryside, he gradually overcame his dependency on Corot and Courbet and, as demonstrated in this picture, established an intimacy with nature that permitted him — in the words of a contemporary — "to see and render a country lane as if it were a member of his family."

While still reminiscent of the Barbizon School in its rather restrained color scheme and in the careful handling of the brush, *Path by the River* already fully reveals Pissarro's extraordinary sense of structural design. Because of this quality which probably is the most outstanding characteristic of his art, he is considered the link between Corot and Cézanne. Choosing an upright format, relatively rare in landscape painting, the artist has used a complex composition to record the simple beauty of the scene and to recreate its mood: the road, which appears in the left foreground, turns and follows the river as it runs diagonally toward the right background; at the left of the river wooded hills form a gentle curve, while at the right young poplars and a house with a pointed roof accentuate the vertical in a staccato movement. A few figures — a couple walking toward the right and a lady with a parasol proceeding in the opposite direction — emphasize the spaciousness of the site. The gloriously painted sky, which rises high above the landscape and occupies half of the picture, sets the mood of the scene and inundates it with the light and air that anticipate Pissarro's impressionist works.

Varengeville, Auberge du Manoir, Gray Day, painted thirty-five years later at a hamlet near Dieppe, sums up the various phases of Pissarro's development. Juxtaposing it with *Path by the River,* it becomes evident that despite the conspicuous differences in technique and color, fundamental aspects of Pissarro's style remained consistent and his relationship to nature unchanged. In

79 PATH BY THE RIVER
(Near La Varenne-St.-Hilaire)   1864
Oil on canvas; 22 x 18 inches
Signed and dated lower right: *C. Pissarro. 1864*
The Maryland Institute, George A. Lucas Collection
On Indefinite Loan to
The Baltimore Museum of Art

80 VARENGEVILLE, AUBERGE DU MANOIR,
GRAY DAY 1899
Oil on canvas; 26 x 21 1/2 inches
Signed and dated lower left: *C. Pissarro 99*
Lent by the Cincinnati Art Museum

Varengeville, as in practically all his landscapes, the artist has selected a humble subject and endowed it with poetry. Although here the intricate arrangement of his early composition has been greatly simplified, the same structural clarity prevails.

Much more obvious than these constant elements of Pissarro's art are the differences with the early work. *Varengeville* exemplifies the old impressionist artist's concern with light and movement and their effects on his subject. Freed from what he came to consider the shackles of neo-impressionism, Pissarro in his late works enjoyed his regained spontaneity. Although the manner in which the color has been applied might recall his previous involvement with pointillism, the brush strokes are no longer evenly and meticulously put on the canvas; here their calligraphy has been accelerated to a kind of speed writing by which the entire surface of the scene seems to have been set in motion.

G. R.

Pierre-Auguste Renoir
French, 1841-1919

It is significant that when a title was being sought for the first group exhibition of impressionist paintings held at Nadar's in 1874, Renoir insisted that no specific term be used which would act as a label unifying the participating members into a new school of painting in the minds of public and critics alike (Rewald, 1961, p. 313). Renoir counted Monet and Sisley among his closest friends and on various occasions in the late 1860's and early 1870's worked alongside Monet in front of nature, attacking the pictorial problem of representing the action of light in landscape and developing similar and often identical painterly techniques. Although there is no question that Renoir's paintings, and especially the landscapes of this period, fall within the scholarly definitions of impressionism, his basic attitudes and his succeeding stylistic development from the 1880's on set him apart. Late in his career he told Vollard that he had "wrung Impressionism dry" by 1883. "I finally came to the conclusion that I knew neither how to paint nor how to draw. In a word, Impressionism was a blind alley as far as I was concerned. . ." (Pach, 1950, p. 18).

Renoir never thought of himself as a revolutionary but rather as a product of a long tradition beginning with the Renaissance and including some of his immediate predecessors. During the 1860's and early 1870's he experimented with a number of approaches and painterly methods discovered in other artists' works. Unsure of which direction he wanted to go, unhappy with anything even slightly methodical, essentially a romantic in temperament and possessing a tremendous technical facility, Renoir found it natural and rewarding to shift back and forth in style from one picture to another, and often within one picture itself (Rewald, 1961, p. 162).

Child with Hoop reveals a combination of techniques typical of his early pictures. Brush strokes vary from the fine strands of paint which appear in the child's head and arms, to the medium-sized strokes found in the chair to the left, to the very broadly applied paint which forms the black dress, to the fairly thick splotches of impasto in the ruffled blouse and in the oriental carpet. The rounded forms of the child's head and arms contrast sharply with the flatness of the black dress which is reminiscent of Manet. There are aspects of the picture which are related to the impressionist methods being developed by Monet and Renoir at this time. Renoir has combined his interest in the action of light on skin and

81   CHILD WITH HOOP   c.1875
Oil on canvas: 24 1/4 x 19 1/4 inches
Signed lower right: *Renoir*
The Abram Eisenberg Collection
On Indefinite Loan to
The Baltimore Museum of Art

hair with his desire to capture a particular physiognomy and personality. The brilliantly light-filled areas of the face and arms lend a sensation of vitality and immediacy to the canvas, which is further enhanced by the gradual merging of one color area into another so that no firm divisions between forms appear. On the other hand, Renoir has chosen to place his figure in an indoor setting, which the plein-airists such as Monet and Sisley rarely used, but which Renoir preferred for his portraits even during his most impressionist phase. He has created shadows — in the red chair especially — through the traditional method of lowering the value and intensity of the local color by adding black, a concept to which the impressionists were diametrically opposed.

Around 1900 Renoir developed arthritis

and moved to southern France where the warm climate made life easier for him. Forced into a wheelchair in 1912, he was nevertheless undaunted by his physical sufferings and continued to devote himself passionately to his art. John Rewald (1961, pp. 580, 584) has written movingly of the achievements of these late years, embodied in such works as *Portrait of Mme. Renoir.* "Manifesting a particular preference for red, from the pinkish red of flesh to the purplish red of roses, he delighted in retaining the fluidity of living forms in a large array of red nuances, modeling volumes with subtle strokes, an expression of his immense knowledge as well as of his ingenuity and eternal freshness. . . . Like Cézanne,

Renoir achieved in his last years the synthesis of his lifelong experience. Impressionism lay far behind him; he retained merely the glistening texture of it, yet the shimmering surface of pigment he used now not to render atmospheric effects but to build with brilliant and strong colors an image of life in almost supernatural intensity. . . . In attaining the balance between observation and vision, the aging Renoir created a new style, crowning his works by a series of masterpieces, exalted in color, subtle in rhythm, forceful in volumes and rich in invention, progressing from canvas to canvas with fertile imagination and happy renditions."

Diana F. Johnson

82 PORTRAIT OF MADAME RENOIR c.1910
Oil on canvas; 32 x 25 5/8 inches
Signed lower left: *Renoir*
Lent by the Wadsworth Atheneum
The Ella Gallup Sumner and
Mary Catlin Sumner Collection

John Singer Sargent
American, 1856-1925

Born of American parents whose life was an unending Grand Tour, John Singer Sargent was one of the breed of nineteenth-century American expatriate artists. Early recognizing their son's talents, Sargent's parents in 1874 had entered him in the studio of Carolus-Duran, a popular portrait painter and member of the French Academy. Sargent was strongly affected by the spontaneous brushwork and rich pigmentation of his master's bravura technique, and like Carolus, impressed by the work of Courbet, Manet and such Spanish baroque artists as Velázquez. He seems also to have adopted Carolus' belief that portraiture was the key to success, and that the maintenance of one's position rested upon never going beyond the rules of form erected by the "establishment." An apt pupil, Sargent gradually built a reputation as one of the most fashionable portrait painters in both Europe and the United States.

While as a portrait painter he presented to the world the image of a congenial and sociable man who enjoyed the material benefits of public acceptance, Sargent nurtured within a private sensitivity which led him to create landscapes, genre and informal portraits, far more intimate and — ultimately for him — far more rewarding than his public commissions. Throughout his career, in such works as *The Oyster Gatherers of Cancale* and *Two Girls Fishing*, he exhibited his love for genre scenes set in landscape, which from 1909 until his death constituted the greater part of his oeuvre.

The Oyster Gatherers of Cancale, painted when Sargent was twenty-two, received an Honorable Mention in the *Salon* of 1878. Although the direct brushwork may reflect the methods of Carolus-Duran, the luminous and translucent qualities of the paint —

83 THE OYSTER GATHERERS OF CANCALE 1878
Oil on canvas; 31 1/8 x 48 1/2 inches
Signed, inscribed and dated lower right:
JOHN S. SARGENT/ PARIS 1878
Lent by The Corcoran Gallery of Art

which cause the atmosphere to shimmer, the puddles to glisten and surfaces of clothing and skin to give forth light — reveal Sargent's awareness of contemporaneous impressionist developments. He had met Claude Monet in 1876 and formed a close friendship with him which was to prove longlasting, but he was never able to commit himself totally to the impressionist cause which effected a separation of these artists from their critics and public. However, his attraction to their ideas coupled with his simultaneous rejection of their radical technical discoveries can be seen in such pictures as *The Oyster Gatherers*.

While after his death Sargent's work was criticized for being all technique and no substance, the two paintings in this exhibition reveal his continuous concern for spatial construction within calculatedly informal organizations. He repeats shapes,

contours and directions in the overall structure and again in smaller details to achieve an interrelationship of parts which joins figures with landscape. The unity of structure is counterbalanced by the evanescent light effects in *The Oyster Gatherers* and by the brushwork in *Two Girls Fishing* whereby the paint, more thickly and rapidly applied, takes on a life of its own, separate from the natural forms it is supposed to represent.

Even though Sargent was not fundamentally an innovator and in his commissioned portraits occasionally yielded to the tastes of his patrons, he sustained a poetic vision and demonstrated his increasing awareness that it was his private world which provided him with his greatest opportunities for personal expression.

Diana F. Johnson

84 TWO GIRLS FISHING 1912
Oil on canvas; 22 x 28 1/4 inches
Signed and dated lower right:
John S. Sargent 1912
Lent by the Cincinnati Art Museum

Henri de Toulouse-Lautrec
French, 1864-1901

85   PORTRAIT OF JEANNE WENZ   1886
Oil on canvas; 32 x 23 1/4 inches
Signed lower right: *HT-Lautrec*
Lent by The Art Institute of Chicago
Gift of Annie Swan Coburn to the
Mr. and Mrs. Lewis L. Coburn Memorial Collection

Both in the subjects he chose to paint and the manner in which he interpreted them, Toulouse-Lautrec has generally been associated with the realist-impressionist tradition. Already as a child he had embraced the world of actualities, observing the manners and movements of the people around him and recording them with an irrepressible instinct for caricature and a precocious mastery of line. Before he had ever seen a Manet or a Degas or watched Renoir paint or formed his admiration for Forain or matriculated in the Ecole des Beaux Arts, he had learned to select the precisely appropriate detail, to paint in planes of light, and to articulate the transitory gesture, so that the effect of his contact with the older masters seems less a matter of sudden illumination or education than an outgrowth of innate proclivities.

The *Portrait of Jeanne Wenz* was painted shortly after Lautrec, discontented with academic pretension, pomposity and sentiment, had detached himself from Cormon's studio. While there is much in the work that would be preserved or developed in succeeding years — the concentration on the head, the subtle delineation of the profile, the manner in which one shape responds to another — the picture is still essentially descriptive, the broken tones and Forainesque cross-hatching establishing volume in space and suggesting the play of light and atmosphere.

Lautrec's style was to remain to the very end firmly grounded in objective reality, but it acquired its particular flavor and potency from an admixture of methods more frequently associated with symbolist abstraction than with realist observation. From the time he entered Cormon's studio he had allied himself with the young painters who, in one way or another, were contributing to the development and definition of the symbolist aesthetic, at Cormon's with Anquetin, Bernard and van Gogh, later on with Bonnard, Vuillard and the other nabis. Like them he rejected traditional modes of composition and developed a style based on the free manipulation of the pictorial means, in which the logic of the picture plane took precedence over the logic of

86 THE OPERA MESSALINA
AT BORDEAUX 1900-01
Oil on canvas; 39 x 28 1/2 inches
Monogrammed lower left: *HTL*
Lent by The Los Angeles County Museum of Art
Mr. and Mrs. George Gard De Sylva Collection

external space and light. The result was a new kind of visual metaphor illustrated by one of Lautrec's last works, representing Messalina descending the stairs.

Messalina was a Roman empress who had the instincts of a praying mantis: insatiably voracious, she took many lovers and, after loving, killed them. Like Wilde's *Salomé* and Mallarmé's *Herodias,* like the prurient priests of Félicien Rops, Messalina was well suited to feed the *fin de siècle* appetite for perversity. In the six paintings he executed on the theme, however, Lautrec was not, in the manner of the academy, reconstructing antiquity, but was rather depicting scenes from an opera by Isidore de Lara presented in Bordeaux in 1900 and apparently never revived. The world of entertainment was Lautrec's milieu. He approached it, however, not as a simple fan, nor as a mere chronicler of mores. In gin mill and café concert, in theater or brothel, at the racetrack or the opera ball, facets of the human psyche, disguised in the formal rituals of the *haute monde* and the heroics and sentimentality of the academy, came into sharper focus. There he could discover the deeper psychological truths that fascinated him and so many others of his time and make of the artificial a symbol of the real. The method he developed was quite personal: he discarded the internal consistency found in his early work and assembled what might be described as clusters of evocative stimuli.

In *Messalina* the massive volumes of the gross figure in the foreground oppose the flattened forms of Messalina herself, while the chorus lacks substance altogether. In one place color sculptures form, in another it suggests light, and generally it helps to define space; but the red will not hold its place in depth and lies on the surface plane like pools and drops of blood. Movement and drama are as much in the color, shapes and lines, and the relationships among them, as in the pantomime of the figures represented. Messalina descends the stairs not by means of the articulated action of her body — which is two-dimensional in any case — but by means of the blunted, arrow-like form that points her downward; and drama is conveyed through the contrasts of dark and light, curved and straight, volume and plane, large and small. The mature style, in short, combines realist volume and impressionist light with symbolist abstraction. The implications of the synthesis were quickly grasped by Lautrec's admirers in the younger generation, among them Braque and Picasso.

Lincoln Johnson

Joseph Mallord William Turner

British, 1775-1851

87   THE FIFTH PLAGUE OF EGYPT   1800
Oil on canvas; 49 x 72 inches
Lent by The Art Association of Indianapolis
Herron Museum of Art

The critic who wrote in 1819 of imagination and reality striving for mastery in Turner's works was in no doubt that reality was suffering a lamentable defeat. It is evident that both the kind of reality and the order of imagination that painting had traditionally offered were changing in Turner's hands. . . . *The Fifth Plague of Egypt* [exhibited when Turner was twenty-five] is a grand imaginative invention . . . Impressions of a storm in the mountains of North Wales were grafted onto the style of Poussin to make a formidable manifestation of the Sublime — the representation in Burke's words, of "whatever is in any sort terrible." Turner's natural sense of awe had become linked with his ambition and his sense of style. We do not think of sheer ambition as a particularly creative or sympathetic quality in an artist, but in Turner it was surely both. . . . *The Fifth Plague,* which actually represented the Seventh, for Turner had no particular interest in any part of the Bible but the Apocalypse, was the first of his great gestures of emulation. The equation of the weather of North Wales with the thunder and hail and the fire that ran along the ground was the beginning of a long engrossment in the force of nature. In the years that followed, Turner was, in fact, compiling a collection both of overwhelming natural effects and of compelling artistic styles. The hostile power of nature provided a series of subjects . . . But he gave an equal force to his other theme, the pictures of fair prospects. In combination the two were irresistible. Light and the elements were not only Turner's subjects; they were his as allies in carrying everything before him.

. . . In the pictures that Turner showed — and concealed — in the last two decades of his life a change was evidently taking place of a kind that is disturbing to an artist's public. . . . The grandeur of Turner's later

88 MERCURY SENT
TO ADMONISH AENEAS c.1850
Oil on canvas; 35 1/2 x 47 1/2 inches
Lent by The Trustees of The Tate Gallery

painting is different in kind from the impressiveness of earlier years. . . Perhaps the whole essence of Turner's last works might be gathered from the compound, infinite meanings that he gave to water. It was not only, more often than not, his subject; it was in many senses his medium. Water typified the world as he imagined it, a world of rippling, echoing light. . . . Water gave some of its meaning to watercolour. The wetness of the medium had fateful connotations. The colour of clouds, and eventually all colour, soaked out into it, bleeding and drowning. The uncontrollable hazards of watercolour were the medium of Turner's private imaginative life. He was at home with them and trusted them, just as he trusted the rich, capricious deposit of oil paint. He made the chance and fate of painting his fate; he was content to abide by it. The diaphanous, yet strangely violent tissue of the last paintings holds a profound confidence and courage, a faithful agreement to conditions that are inherent not only in painting but in the whole irrevocable order of the material world.

Mercury Sent to Admonish Aeneas was one of Turner's last four pictures, all of Carthaginian subjects, exhibited in the year before his death. . . It shows the serene solution of his style. . . As colour becomes visible, it dilates on the canvas. The halation diffuses, tingeing the next, until every hue is present in every other, enriching yet also destroying. There is an illusion that colour is gathering in awesome caverns, places of simultaneous reconcilation and annihilation. This is Turner's conclusion, and it justifies Ruskin's insight: ". . . Here and there, once in a couple of centuries, one man will rise past clearness and become dark with excess of light." *

Lawrence Gowing

*Selected from L. Gowing, *Turner: Imagination and Reality,* 1966. All rights reserved by The Museum of Modern Art, New York.

James Abbott McNeill Whistler
American, 1834-1903

89 AT THE PIANO c.1858
Oil on canvas; 26 3/8 x 36 1/2 inches
Signed lower left: *Whistler*
Lent by The Taft Museum
Louise Taft Semple Bequest

"As music is the poetry of sound, so painting is the poetry of sight, and the subject matter has nothing to do with the harmony of sound or of color."

It is not surprising that an American of Puritan background such as Whistler should have been attracted to the realist position of Courbet and his circle. And it was propitious that the young Whistler's arrival in Paris in 1855 should have coincided with Courbet's famous one-man show, "Le Réalisme, G. Courbet." It is always difficult to measure the influence exerted by one artist upon another, but it appears certain that it was Courbet's example that led Whistler to affirm his own individuality and independence as an artist, to settle upon familiar subject matter and to explore the poetic possibilities of mood and atmosphere. The realists, of course, acknowledged their debt to their great models of the seventeenth century, and in Whistler's work, too, one can detect the influence of Velázquez Ribera, Hals and Rembrandt.

At the Piano, painted only three years after Whistler's arrival in Europe, was the artist's first major work and embodies nearly all those elements of composition and color which later were to be refined into that uniquely Whistlerian style which constitutes a singularly personal contribution to western painting. This painting depicts Whistler's elder half-sister Deborah and her daughter Annie. In a quiet domestic moment the subjects are withdrawn into a private world with an atmosphere of its own. The paint surface is thick and rich, the construction forceful in its sharp juxtaposition of verticals and horizontals, lights and darks. Yet the picture is not harsh or jarring; it is balanced compositionally and tonally by the artist's extremely careful attention to the total harmony of color and design.

In later years Whistler's brush became less heavily loaded, his sensitivity to color more refined and his articulation of space more abstract as he came under the influence of oriental art. With maturity he developed a

90 GOLD AND BROWN: SELF PORTRAIT c.1900
Oil on canvas; 24 1/2 x 18 1/4 inches
Signed with butterfly right center
Lent by the National Gallery of Art
Washington, D. C.
Gift of Edith Stuyvesant Gerry

heightened sense of individuality and intro-spection, and although he had learned much from the realists, he finally rejected Courbet, saying he wished he might have studied with Ingres. The one constant enthusiasm throughout his life was for Velázquez, and it was an enthusiasm that served him well. In both oriental and hellenistic art he found elements which he used to enhance the tonal and compositional aspects of his work, and he sought always to attain his personal vision of perfection through a re-fined elegance.

Gold and Brown: Self Portrait is, in a way, not wholly characteristic of Whistler's last years, for it is a forceful work from a time when the artist's strength had begun to decline. It seems to represent Whistler in a searching moment during which he makes a final, telling statement about him-self and his art. The existence of two other versions of this painting serves not only to illustrate Whistler's methods, but also to indicate how important this portrait must have been for him. It is a painting distin-guished by its characterization and percep-tion, realized through great economy of means. The head is modeled with a fluid pigment applied in sure, broad areas of light and shadow, while the color range of browns and golds is very narrow. The sub-ject's attitude is at once both insistently disdainful and curiously withdrawn, as if the artist were purposefully presenting an enigma which he dares the viewer to de-fine.

As one of Whistler's last statements on portraiture, and perhaps on art as well, it is tempting to compare such a work with the late self portraits of Rembrandt and Courbet. The strong thread of realistic tradition cer-tainly connects all three. In such highly personal works, however, it is the unique vision of the artist which goes farthest in explaining the excellence of such paintings. In Whistler's case the vision becomes ex-ceedingly rarefied in its transference to can-vas, and reality appears so abstracted that the subject loses its material significance to the poetic shadow of reality.

"As the light fades and the shadows deepen all petty and exacting details vanish, every-thing trivial disappears, and I see things as they are in great strong masses: the buttons are lost, but the sitter remains; the gar-ment is lost, but the sitter remains; the sitter is lost, but the shadow remains; the shadow is lost, but the picture remains. And that, night cannot efface from the painter's imagination."

John A. Mahey

Max Beckmann
German, 1884-1950

Beckmann grew up in Braunschweig, and as a young man he admired the works by Rembrandt in the Herzog Anton Ulrich Museum there. Indeed, no artist since Rembrandt has examined his own physiognomy with such penetration as Max Beckmann. For fifty years he was engaged in a continuous search for self. He painted numerous self portraits, holding a mirror before his face, seeking his identity and studying his reaction to the world and the world's estimate of his own personality. In these paintings Beckmann has seen himself as performer, conjurer and mountebank — he is the active conscience of his time, but he is also the victim afflicted by fate. Like the actor, capable of living a variety of lives by means of dramatic ritual, Beckmann, too, assumes a multiplicity of masks to observe and act in the human drama, where truth is intermingled with illusion.

The early *Self Portrait* is a romantic vision of the artist looking out at the world with brusque affirmation. A young man still in his twenties, Beckmann was already eminently successful: his large ambitious history paintings, done in dark colors but with a vigorous brush, had earned him acclaim as the "German Delacroix"; he could look back on a number of one-man shows; a monograph had just been written on his work; and he was lauded as the most promising young artist in Germany.

The experience of the war, in which he served as a medical corpsman, transformed his life and his work. Confronted with the wounded and the dying, Beckmann found that only by making drawings, by giving a tangible and visual expression to his experience, could he keep going. From a realism with all the undertones of *belle peinture*, he turned to a verism which looked straight in the face of reality. No longer satisfied with describing what things look like, Beckmann began to concern himself with what really happens, and he rendered the spectacle with cold and restrained sobriety. Beckmann was never an expressionist painter.

After making a new start in Frankfurt, having lived in Paris and Berlin between the wars, Beckmann went into voluntary exile in 1934, the day after Hitler opened the Great German Art exhibition at the Haus der Deutschen Kunst in Munich. Simultaneously ten of Beckmann's paintings were shown at the Degenerate Art exhibition there. Beckmann moved to Amsterdam where he was to live in isolation and work quietly and magnificently for ten years.

His isolation was never total: there were a few friends, a few fellow exiles, and *Four*

91 SELF PORTRAIT 1912
Oil on canvas; 18 x 17 inches
Signed and dated upper right: *Beckmann/ 12*
Lent by Mr. and Mrs. Allan Frumkin

Men Around a Table gives visual evidence of his life among his emigrant friends in Holland. He is seated at the table on the lower right with the painter Friedrich Vordemberge-Gildewart, who had arrived in Amsterdam in 1938, at his left. The man with the high cap on the upper left is the painter Herbert Fiedler, and above Beckmann is Ludwig Berger, the theater director. His friends have brought edibles to their secret meeting — a turnip, a fish and a loaf of bread — while Beckmann himself holds a mirror which reflects his own visage. Seated in silence around the table with its brightly burning candles (a candle may symbolize its own consumption as well as hope) are four men who seem to have come together for a significant and festive occasion, the particular purpose of which remains a mystery. The attributes of the four men do not help in the interpretation, because

Beckmann always maintained ambiguity in his paintings. Beckmann set out to communicate a general feeling, to express truths which are put into visual, not verbal terms. The feeling here, as in most of his mature works, is largely derived from the strength of his potent shapes, the sonorous quality of his color, and above all, from his handling of space: the four men are crowded together in the confining space of a room which seems too small to contain them. Against the frightening onslaught of the void, Max Beckmann fills all available space, but significantly he occupies it here with friends, in whose company the solitary artist found temporary consolation during the dark years of war and isolation.

Peter Selz

92   FOUR MEN AROUND A TABLE   1943
Oil on canvas; 58 3/8 x 45 1/2 inches
Signed and dated lower center: *Beckmann/ A 43*
Lent from the Collection of
Washington University

George Wesley Bellows

American, 1882-1925

93 SUMMER NIGHT — RIVERSIDE DRIVE 1909
Oil on canvas; 35 1/2 x 47 1/2 inches
Signed lower center: *Geo. Bellows*
Lent by the Columbus Gallery of Fine Arts
Frederick W. Schumacher Collection

It may seem absurd to talk about "early" and "late" in the career of a man who died at forty-two, but by that age George Bellows had been painting for a long time. Everyone is so appalled by his early death that one forgets to be grateful for his early start. Prodigies are rare in American art, but the paintings Bellows did in his twenties are among his very best.

Summer Night — Riverside Drive is a hymn to night and the city and to the great park along the Hudson. It was, in those days, a haven of romance and poetry, and even now it is one of the most spectacular parts of town. To men from west of the Alleghenies, the water around New York is a perpetual astonishment. Bellows' boyhood rivers were the Scioto and the Olen-

tangy, which meet in Columbus, his old home town, and he was overcome by the Hudson and painted it many, many times. New York is a curiously inward-looking city, considering that it is surrounded by waterways that rival those of San Francisco. *Summer Night — Riverside Drive* is one of Bellows' few night pictures, and it deserves to be called a nocturne, with the breeze making the lights sparkle on the water. These early pictures have the dark tones he learned from his teacher Henri; the color is low in key, out of Munich and Holland.

The Picnic lies at the other edge of color and of the artist's career. Bellows was very much interested in the craft of painting, and he was strongly affected by writers such as Denman Ross, who made a detailed

94 THE PICNIC 1924
Oil on canvas; 30 1/8 x 44 1/4 inches
Signed lower left: *Geo. Bellows*
The Peabody Institute, Irwin Fund
On Indefinite Loan to
The Baltimore Museum of Art

study of sixty different color-palettes; some of the canvases Bellows painted under his shadow were limited to a few colors, others were painted with the rainbow. For many of his paintings he used colors recommended by Hardesty Maratta, another theorist of the time. It is difficult to exaggerate the colorfulness of the American countryside, and in *The Picnic* the new tonalities worked to their best advantage; at other times the result is close to disaster. In compositional matters he deferred to Jay Hambidge, apostle of a doctrine called "Dynamic Symmetry," which Bellows regarded as "prob-ably more valuable than the study of anatomy." Hambidge's influence upon Bellows was paramount until the end of his life. If these hills and figures seem strangely placed, it is because they were placed there by the painter's mind, not his eye.

Bellows was a prodigious worker; one glorious October in Maine he painted forty-two canvases. With such energy and talent, it is impossible to tell where this bright hope of American painting might have gone.

Mahonri Sharp Young

Pierre Bonnard
French, 1867-1947

95 LUNCHEON TABLE 1897-99
Oil on board; 19 1/2 x 25 3/4 inches
Signed lower right: *Bonnard*
The Baltimore Museum of Art
Frederic W. Cone Bequest

Bonnard thought of himself as the last of the impressionists. His iridescent color structures bear little resemblance, however, to those impressionist pictures which transfer the retinal image to the canvas; they have more in common with the work his friends Monet and Renoir produced at the end of the century and after, when color seems as much invented as observed, and concern with line and spatial construction take on greater importance than they had before.

At the beginning of his career Bonnard operated in an aesthetic field somewhat removed from impressionism. Like the other members of the nabis group, *le nabis japonard,* as he was called, participated in the symbolist search for ways of translating feeling into form and developed a style nurtured not only by impressionism, but by Gauguin, the Japanese printmakers and art nouveau designers as well. If he absorbed some impressionist methods — the accentuated attack, the suppression of descriptive detail, the representation of volume by plane — he used them for quite different ends than the impressionists did. As if responding to Maurice Denis' reminder that

a painting is, first of all, a flat plane covered with tones arranged in a certain order, he stressed surface patterns in which each part seems to have equivalent value, and persons and objects often lose their identity in the design. Decorative arabesques, embroidered surfaces and clearly defined forms arranged parallel to the picture plane characterize his art at this time. Frequently, too, there are bold contrasts of value and a daring disposition of shapes; but the generally neutralized tonality and the matte surface, resulting from the use of distemper as a medium or oil-absorbing board as a support, invest the works with a reticence and quiet that seem entirely consonant with the subject matter, the intimate life of the bourgeois.

The *Luncheon Table* seems to have been painted in the late nineties, when Bonnard's style was gaining greater complexity. The suppressed conflict between volume and plane and between deep space and surface pattern was becoming intensified, but the brushwork remains indeterminate rather than descriptive, and the forms it so imprecisely suggests reveal their identity only momentarily, then mysteriously disappear into the pattern again, like the dog and the boy who can be faintly discerned through the doorway.

Throughout his career Bonnard's approach was to shift almost rhythmically — and almost imperceptibly — as he tried to maintain a delicate balance between the volume and the plane, the highly structured space and the sumptuous richness of tone, impressionist observation and symbolist abstraction, reality and dream. The impression he paints, then, is not so much of things perceived as feelings evoked. Nowhere is this more evident than in his depictions of white tablecloths, or the white tiles and porcelains of the bathroom he was finally able to provide for his wife Marthe. Nacreous, iridescent, painted as if seen through a spectrum, cloth and tile lose their substance to become pure, jewel-like light. Such interior luminosity originates in the subtle control of contrast, which Bonnard may well have learned from Seurat's neo-impressionist followers. Although barely apparent in *The Luncheon Table*, it characterizes most of his mature work and is illustrated in the *Self Portrait* of 1938, in which the surface is enlivened and enriched not only by the bold contrasts of light and dark and warm and cool, but also by the delicate differentiation of white and yellow.

The portrait is typical of the late style. There is a peculiar duality in the structure, so delicately balanced between the linear and painterly modes: the shapes are clearly defined but the contours imprecise; the volumes are suggested but absorbed by the plane; the straight lines of the architecture are boldly stated but never quite vertical or horizontal or, for that matter, never quite straight; and the tones, except for a few accents, are never quite definable but always tremulously on the verge of becoming something else. And in that dualism, so subtly controlled by his impressionist touch, is not only a mastery of style but an inner vision, which sees the permanent in the transitory and the lyrical in the banal.

Lincoln Johnson

96 SELF PORTRAIT 1938
Oil on canvas; 23 x 26 3/8 inches
Signed lower right: *Bonnard*
Lent by Wildenstein and Co., Inc

Georges Braque
French, 1882-1963

Braque was the last, but by no means the least, recruit to fauvism. After his eyes were opened by "the novelty, physical excitement, youthfulness, paroxysmal qualities" of the fauves at the *Salon d'Automne* in 1906, he jettisoned half-hearted impressionism, the style of his very beginnings.

Braque's earliest extant works in the fauve idiom date from the summer of 1906, when he and Othon Friesz went to Antwerp. The composition of the Antwerp views is banal and the fauvism tentative. However, in the winter of 1906-07 which Braque spent at L'Estaque, a small port near Marseilles, he rapidly developed a style of his own. He adjusted his palette to the light and color

of the Mediterranean scene and experimented with new ways of rendering space. After a stay in Paris, where he met Matisse and his cohorts, Braque returned to the Mediterranean — this time to La Ciotat. Later in the year he went back to L'Estaque, where he painted the work included in this exhibition.

Braque's landscapes of 1907 established him not only as a leading fauve, but also as one of the most progressive painters of his generation. Disdaining the theory of Matisse, the virtuosity of Derain and the vulgarity of Vlaminck, Braque evolved a personal and characteristically painterly approach to fauvism. Following Cézanne, who

97 L'ESTAQUE 1907
Oil on canvas; 31 3/8 x 27 3/4 inches
Signed on back
Lent from the Collection of
Colonel Samuel A. Berger

had also painted at L'Estaque, he used color — half tones as well as primaries — to build up form rather than to indicate the play of light, never employing color decoratively or as an end in itself. *L'Estaque,* one of Braque's strongest fauve works, renounces deep recession in its spatial organization and anticipates his landscapes painted the following year which were the first pictures to be termed "cubist."

Toward the end of his life, Braque's approach to art became ever more equivocal and visionary. "Art and Life have become one," he said, "objects don't exist for me except insofar as a *rapport* exists between them, or between them and myself." His impressive series of *Ateliers* (1949-56) are the ultimate expression of these ideas, but reflections of them are to be found in most of his post-war works including *The Sunflowers* of 1957. Also, instead of limiting an object in a picture to one specific identity, Braque liked to paint things as if they were in a state of flux — what he called "metamorphosis." Thus, certain forms have two or three meanings, others none at all; they are "rhymes" or accidents that the artist has incorporated into his picture (e.g. the small triangle above the sunflowers).

This flower-piece is "metamorphic" by virtue of the possible changes indicated in white. For the period of this picture's gestation in the studio, these notations existed in white chalk — a favorite device of the artist. By retaining them in the more permanent medium of oil paint, Braque implies that, far from having come to a halt, the creative process could be carried still further. Much as Braque disliked finishing his work, *The Sunflowers* should not be regarded as unfinished, but as a painting still in a state of transition. The artist has involved the beholder directly with his work and enabled him to assume — at least in imagination — the role of painter. The apparent subject of these late works is little more than a pretext; the true subject is painting itself.

John Richardson

98 THE SUNFLOWERS 1957
Oil on board; 23 3/8 x 24 3/8 inches
Signed lower center: *G. Braque*
Lent by Mr. and Mrs. Gustave Ring

Marc Chagall
Russian (French School), 1887-

Marc Chagall painted *I and the Village* the year after he first arrived in Paris from his native Russia, intent on establishing himself as an artist. His Russian background has formed a basic source of his art throughout his career, but the works of his first years in Paris reflected most strongly a nostalgic longing for his homeland. "The fact that I made use of cows, milkmaids, roosters and provincial Russian architecture as my source forms is because they are part of the environment from which I spring and which undoubtedly left the deepest impression on my visual memory of any experience I have known. Every painter is born somewhere. And even though he may later turn to the influences of other atmospheres, a certain essence — a certain 'aroma' — of his birthplace clings to the work" (Statement by Chagall quoted in Liberman, 1955, p. 121).

The rustic, poetic imagery, rich color, and almost ritualistic, dream-like mood of *I and the Village* are of the artist's personal invention and are found in practically all of his later work. His use of color is not naturalistic, but directed instead toward emotional expressiveness. Perspective-projection is replaced by a device common in medieval illuminations, that of giving greatest size to the most important features in the picture. While all these factors can be traced back to Chagall's Russian beginnings, the handling of composition in *I and the Village* exhibits his exposure to the new "atmosphere" of the Paris world where cubism was flourishing. At no other time in his career was Chagall so concerned with the tight structural organization of the canvas in order to emphasize its surface plane. Forms are flattened out and are clearly integrated into an overall surface pattern with predominant circular and triangular shapes operating almost independently of the images portrayed.

Fundamentally opposed to cubism and its concern for objectivity, he soon eliminated from his paintings the vestiges of cubist compositional techniques. Nevertheless, the discipline which cubism had exerted upon him during the brief years before the outbreak of World War I was the very factor which enabled Chagall later to work successfully, in such paintings as *Le Peintre Amoureux*, in a style marked by a freedom of composition, brushwork and color.

Despite its freedom of execution, *Le Peintre Amoureux* was worked on over a period of eight years, a not uncommon occurrence in Chagall's oeuvre. "I could do ten paintings a day, like some of the others, if I wanted to. It's not that hard to paint

99 I AND THE VILLAGE 1911
Oil on canvas; 75 5/8 x 59 5/8 inches
Signed and dated lower left:
Chagall/ 1911 Paris
Lent by The Museum of Modern Art, New York
Mrs. Simon Guggenheim Fund

and sign a picture. But there's more to it than that. A true work of art is a self-contained world, and the world wasn't made in a day. . . . I do believe things must arrive at their finish naturally and normally. . ." (Lake, 1958, p. 72).

The lovers of *Le Peintre Amoureux* evolve from a theme begun in 1915, when Chagall painted the first of his pictures celebrating the major events in his married life. Like Picasso, he has always revealed in his work his deep love for women and the major role they have played in his life. In this painting the artist-lover is loosely coupled with his bride in a tender, almost bashful relationship. They are the pivotal image around which all the lesser symbols of love and happiness glide, seeming to move to the festive music provided by an airborne violinist. The only other image which vies with the central couple is the shimmering floral bouquet, which has been present in his art since the mid-1920's, when he was first struck by the beauty of French flowers. But perhaps the most distinguishing features of this and other late works are the glowing color and rich textures which increasingly have become for Chagall the key to expressing life, love and beauty in art. "As you grow older, you become more and more preoccupied with the matière: pigment, color, whatever you want to call it. That's the way it was with Rembrandt. That's the way it was with Renoir. That's what happened with me. I had gradually come to realize that *color is all*. And it was Monet who made me see it. . . . Color is two things. It is chemistry and it is love. Color as love is what so few understand. . . . It's Mozart, it's Watteau, it's children everywhere. It's when you get down on your knees to make a declaration of love or to cry over someone very near to you who has died. . . . It's what we need so badly in the world today, in every sphere — beginning with the political. That's color as love" (Lake, 1958, pp. 72-73).

Diana F. Johnson

100 LE PEINTRE AMOUREUX 1953-61
Oil on canvas; 39 1/4 x 30 5/8 inches
Signed and dated lower right:
Chagall/ Marc 1953-61
Lent by the Perls Galleries

Lovis Corinth
German, 1858-1925

The art of Lovis Corinth joins two distinct cultural epochs — those of nineteenth-century realism and twentieth-century expressionism — without fitting neatly into either. Gifted by nature with immense energy and talent, with powers on the scale of the old masters, and trained in the rigorous conventions of the old academies, Corinth was from the beginning an accomplished but impatient practitioner of these

conventions. The emotions he brought to them were too large and too unruly to conform to the niceties of the academic ideal, particularly as that ideal was envisioned in the Germany of his youth. Yet it was not a disruption of tradition he sought so much as a return to its more vital and extreme resources.

Realism — the realism of Leibl and Courbet — marked his first significant break

**101 PORTRAIT OF FRANZ HEINRICH CORINTH,
THE ARTIST'S FATHER 1888**
Oil on canvas; 46 1/2 x 39 3/8 inches
Signed and dated right center:
Louis Corinth/ Mai 1888
Lent anonymously

with the academic mold. But the specifications of realism could not contain Corinth's passionate energies, which verged at times on the demonic. In the end, he brought painting to the boundaries of expressionism by forcing upon tradition — the tradition of Rembrandt, Hals, Rubens, Velázquez, Courbet and Manet — the exacerbations of feeling smouldering in his soul. For, as it happened, these were the exacerbations smouldering in the soul of the culture he inhabited.

The *Portrait of the Artist's Father,* painted in 1888, is already an indication of the double nature of his talents. The head in this portrait is, without being in the least audacious or risk-taking, a masterly example of the realist style, with its fastidious attention to observed detail and to the character of the sitter. The picture as a whole, however, is virtually "unfinished" — a sketch, as it were, in search of an ampler style to accommodate the artist's full range of feeling.

It was, above all, in the great portraits of his final period that Corinth achieved this ampler style — a style in which the realist fidelity to subject is joined and transcended by a painterly freedom that transforms the entire pictorial surface into an exact visual equivalent of the emotion the artist wishes to convey. *The Black Hussar* is one of the finest examples of this late style in which Corinth effected his most profound synthesis of tradition and personal feeling.

Hilton Kramer

102   THE BLACK HUSSAR   1917
Oil on canvas; 86 1/2 x 47 1/2 inches
Signed and dated upper right:
Lovis Corinth/ 1917
Lent by the Allan Frumkin Gallery

Jean Dubuffet
French, 1901-

103 RHETEUR AU MUR 1945
Oil on canvas; 38 1/4 x 51 1/4 inches
Signed and dated lower left:
J. Dubuffet/ mars 45
The Baltimore Museum of Art
Saidie A. May Collection

"I have liked to carry the human image onto a plane of seriousness where the futile embellishments of aesthetics have no longer any place . . ."

In his rejection of accepted aesthetic tradition, Jean Dubuffet has expressed an attitude common to many twentieth-century artists. In 1945, after having corresponded for some years with patients of insane asylums and their doctors, Dubuffet began his famous collection of *l'art brut* — objects created by persons removed from society, ignorant of the teachings of art schools and unmoved by the forces of fashion in the art world. The intensity and directness of expression in these works, which speak of the mysterious recesses of the mind and its compulsions, held great fascination and inspiration for Dubuffet.

The artistic, emotional and intellectual concerns of this artist are many and are extremely complex. To palpably render the invisible, to dematerialize the physical; to go beyond appearances to the life forces which hover behind and shape existence; to discover the visual means to express the ideas of metamorphosis and regeneration; to reveal the beauty in the banal and the ugly; to juxtapose seeming opposites and thus find relationships that were never thought to exist; to take advantage of chance while maintaining the controlling hand; to find corresponding textures to best match those of living and inert objects; to fuse in his art his simultaneous involvement with external and internal structure, the intangible and the concrete, the universal and the specific — these are the motivating forces behind Dubuffet and his work.

Although he was in his middle years when in the early 1940's he finally devoted himself completely to painting, Dubuffet since that time has produced a prodigious body of work. His stylistic development parallels, to a certain extent, his interest in psychic phenomena and psychotic art. Much as in a dream, images and techniques appear in his work, submerge in the wake of new experiences and discoveries and then reappear later in forms somewhat altered by all that has since transpired. Thus, the stick-like caricatures of urban people, which are present in such early Paris street scenes as *Rheteur au Mur,* disappear for the most part from his paintings of the 1950's. The men and women who do appear in his figurative work of that period are raised to another level of expression. Transformed into totemic images, they are terrifying in their dehumanization, while at the same time they retain in more intense and exaggerated form the grim irony of the early figures.

In 1961 Dubuffet underwent a reversal, reacting negatively to his more recent work and returning, in paintings like *Cote Course Mouche,* to the spirit and methods of his Paris scenes of the forties. The *Rheteur* is presented as a fu'l-length figure seen simultaneously in frontal and profile view; this type reappears in various forms throughout the later painting, with and without hat and tie and often without arms. The figures in *Cote Course Mouche,* however, are not as carefully rendered as those in the earlier pictures and are now combined in far more complex patterns; while in the *Rheteur au Mur* the wall serves as a backdrop for the actor-speaker-demagogue, the figures in *Cote Course Mouche* cannot be distinguished easily from their surroundings, under- and overlapping the intricate webs of impasto which cover the entire surface of the painting. There is now no sense of scale or perspective, and the figures fancifully walk or balance along the sides of the picture. The brilliant colors of the *Rheteur* which are characteristic of Dubuffet's work of the early forties are found in some of his paintings of 1961. Nevertheless, the pervasive lavender-pink-ivory tones as well as the tactile quality of the paint surface in *Cote Course Mouche* are closer to the colors and textures of his works of the fifties.

Despite these stylistic holdovers from his previous work, Dubuffet felt very strongly that his paintings of 1961 were basically very different in conception. In a letter to Peter Selz dated December 21, 1961, Dubuffet wrote: "The principle thing [about my paintings of this year] is that they are in complete contrast to those of the Texturology and Materiology series that I did previously . . . . I believe more and more that my paintings of the previous years avoided in subject and execution specific human motivations. To paint the earth the painter tended to become the earth and to cease to be a man — that is, to be painter. In reaction against this absenteeist tendency my paintings of this year put into play in all respects a very insistent *intervention.* The presence in them of the painter now is constant, even exaggerated. They are full of personages, and this time their role is played with spirit. It seems to me that in the whole development of my work there is a constant fluctuation between bias for personages and bias against them" (Selz, 1962, p. 165).

Diana F. Johnson

104   COTE COURSE MOUCHE   1961
Oil on canvas; 44 1/2 x 57 1/4 inches
Signed and dated lower center:
J. Dubuffet 61
Lent by Mr. and Mrs. Robert E. Meyerhoff

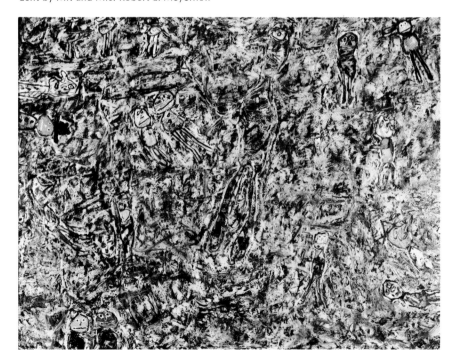

Arshile Gorky
American, 1904-48

Arshile Gorky, whose life was a series of great hardships and tragedies interrupted by brief periods of intense happiness and fulfillment, created in his art a poetic testament to the forces which moved him. If the expressive content of the paintings and drawings of his maturity is deeply personal, the artistic method is in large part a compound of diverse influences accumulated through years of apprenticeship to the art of others. With an unerring eye and infallible taste, he was drawn to the great masters of nineteenth and twentieth-century art, absorbing in sequential order the lessons of post-impressionism through Cézanne, cubism through Picasso, poetic abstract surrealism through Miró, Matta and Breton, and lyrical abstraction through Kandinsky.

In *Organization,* painted during the height of his involvement with cubist ideas, Gorky follows cubist precedent and concentrates on structure and texture, building up his forms in thick layers of paint. Familiar cubist objects like the palette and fruit appear, but already they are translated into a private vocabulary of biomorphic form. Although curvilinear flat shapes combine into a taut interlocking surface pattern, their vitality invest *Organization* with a mystery which is pure Gorky.

In the early 1940's Gorky formed associations with a number of surrealists who had come to the United States during the Euro-

pean upheaval. His dealer, Julien Levy, later wrote about the significance of his encounter with surrealism, which exposed him to the liberating idea of automatism: "For Gorky automatism was a redemption . . . Gorky found meaning with the Surrealists who helped him both to bring himself to the surface and dig himself deep in his work. . . . He found his fantasy legitimatized and discovered that his hidden emotional confusions were not only not shameful but were the mainsprings for his personal statement" (Seitz, 1962, p.8).

In these same years, Gorky, who had always found city life restricting, re-established direct contact with nature during frequent summer visits to his in-laws' farm in Virginia. His joy in observing plant and animal life and his desire to find concrete evocations for his inner imaginings were fused in drawings and paintings remarkable for their freedom of fluid line, glowing color and invention of hybrid formations.

Making the Calendar is the second version of a theme which emerged from the *Fireplace in Virginia* drawings done in the summer of 1946. The first version entitled *The Calendars* (destroyed in the Executive Mansion fire, Albany, 1961) was painted during the winter of 1946-47 and contained within the clearly articulated space of an interior all of the images found in the second version, chief among them the anthro-

105 ORGANIZATION c.1933
Oil on board; 14 1/8 x 22 inches
Signed lower right: *GORKY*
Lent by The University of Arizona Art Gallery
Edward Joseph Gallagher III Memorial Collection

pomorphic rocking chair. While in *The Calendars* Gorky's style was consistent with that of the culminating masterpieces of his career, he reverted in *Making the Calendar* to his earlier 1944-45 style when he was most immersed in the freedom of surrealist automatism. A mobility of forms and paint surfaces free line from color, and thin veils of gray and ochre dissolve and obscure the images in their pulsating rhythms.

To translate Gorky's pictorial vocabulary into a verbal one is to embark upon an exceedingly difficult course, for his imagery is elusive and cryptic. Gorky, a "poet-in-paint" (as his close friend and biographer, Ethel Schwabacher, described him) was interested in the works of literary poets favored by Breton and other surrealists. In the opinion of this writer *Making the Calendar* reveals provocative correspondences with *La Chambre Double,* a prose poem by Charles Baudelaire in which the *poète maudit* describes:

"A room resembling a dream, a really *spiritual* room, . . .

The pieces of furniture have shapes stretched out, prostrate, languid. The pieces of furni-

ture have the air of dreaming; one would say they were endowed with a sleep-walker's life, like the vegetable and the mineral. The materials speak a dumb language like flowers, skies, and setting suns. . .

The faintest fragrance of most exquisite choice to which a very slight humidity is mingled floats in this atmosphere. . .

Muslin rains abundantly in front of the windows and the bed; it pours forth in snowy cascades. On this bed lies the Idol, the sovereign of dreams. . .

There indeed are those eyes whose flame pierces the twilight; those subtle and terrible *optics* that I recognize by their terrifying malice! . . .

O beatitude! what we generally call life has nothing in common, even in its happiest expansion, with this supreme life that I know now and which I taste minute by minute, second by second!

No! there are no more minutes, there are no more seconds! Time has disappeared; it is Eternity which reigns, an eternity of delights! . . ." (Anthony Hartley, trans., 1958, pp. 175-177).

Diana F. Johnson

106 MAKING THE CALENDAR 1947
Oil on canvas; 34 x 41 inches
Signed and dated left center: *A. Gorky/ 47*
Lent by the Munson-Williams-Proctor Institute
Edward W. Root Bequest

Juan Gris
Spanish, 1887-1927

The first known works by Juan Gris are humorous drawings for magazines and illustrations to José Santos Chocano's poems *Alma América,* published in Madrid, 1906. The latter — seventy-one vignettes in the art nouveau manner which Gris had adopted as a result of his friendship with the Munich illustrator Willy Geiger — are usually dismissed as juvenilia. In fact, they are historically important, because they foreshadow Gris' mature style and form a crucial link between German art nouveau and cubism. Specifically, Gris' *Alma América* illustrations anticipate later works in which he abandons perspective and reduces everything to two dimensions; their geometrical stylization, linear organization and homogeneity of design are also prophetic.

After coming to Paris in 1906, Gris began to develop a cubist style of his own. Inevitably the influence of Picasso, his fellow countryman and neighbor in the Bâteau Lavoir, was paramount, but the influence of German illustrators working in the art nouveau style continued to play an important, though less overt, role. In *Roof Tops* this emerges in strong tonal contrasts and abstract dynamism, and also in the way the houses have been assembled into a neat, bottle-shaped configuration.

Comparable cubist views by Picasso and Braque are more equivocal, less rhythmic in organization and, above all, less schematic. Although they admired Gris' work, the two creators of cubism did not altogether hold with his "pictorial calculations." "You had better be careful," Braque once said to Gris, "or one day you are going to find yourself trying to fit two fruit-dishes into a single pear."

In 1925 Gris' health, never good, began seriously to deteriorate, and in 1927 he died. Yet, during these two years his work, which after 1920 had tended to decorative softness (Gris had mistakenly decided to cultivate his "sensitive and sensuous side") entered a powerful new phase of architectonic austerity. Kahnweiler, the artist's biographer and dealer, claims that works dating from this late period — in particular the series of still lifes of which *The Painter's Window* is among the finest — are "the culmination of Gris' work" and "one of the summits of pictorial art." The first claim is more justifiable than the second.

Once again we find Gris deriving strength from his art nouveau roots. The border, which is a recurrent feature of the *Alma América* vignettes, is an integral part of *The Painter's Window* and related compositions. Likewise the fusion of still life objects with

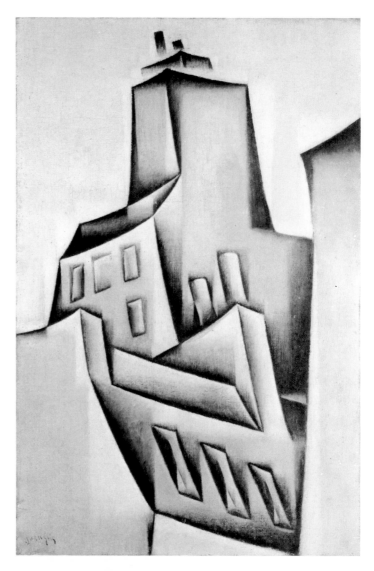

107 ROOF TOPS 1911
Oil on canvas; 20 5/8 x 13 1/2 inches
Signed lower left: *Juan Gris*
Lent by The Solomon R. Guggenheim Museum

108 THE PAINTER'S WINDOW 1925
Oil on canvas; 39 1/4 x 31 3/4 inches
Signed and dated lower left: *Juan Gris . 25*
The Baltimore Museum of Art
Saidie A. May Collection

their setting derives from the same source, as can be seen in the manner in which the top of the guitar is articulated; it is bent back, so that it becomes a window frame, which in turn prolongs itself into the front edge of the table. Furthermore, the simple angular forms in this and similar still lifes are defined, as in the early vignettes, by one or more outlines.

These pictures are not just the artist's swan song; they are the swan song of synthetic cubism. Their coolness and assurance belie the self-doubt and appalling struggle that went into their creation. Far from harking back, their restrained geometry anticipates the work of such contemporary American painters as Frank Stella.

John Richardson

Hans Hofmann
American, 1880-1966

Hans Hofmann painted *Fantasia* in 1943, when he was already sixty-three years old. Even so, this is an "early" work by this master. It is both remarkable and gratifying that in an era of increasing, perhaps unseemly, emphasis on "young" and "fresh" art, Hofmann began his important development only in his sixties and reached his greatest powers only at eighty.

During the early years of this century Hofmann played an active role in the crucial developments and artistic revolutions in both Paris and Munich. He was very close to Henri Matisse and Robert Delaunay in particular; he admired both Kandinsky and Mondrian. He became the great synthesizer and perhaps the most important teacher of his time. Only late in life did he return to painting, because from the time he opened his school in Munich in 1915 until, forty-three years later, he closed it in New York and Provincetown, Hans Hofmann devoted most of his time and creative energies to the demands of his students.

While he shared in contributing an all-important artistic culture to New York, it was in return the vitality and exuberance of the revived art life of that city which largely inspired him to paint again, to test his theories, to explore new territories. Around 1940 Hofmann began to paint with an amazing freedom — freedom even from his own conventions — and created an astonishing diversity of styles. Hofmann was the first American painter to drip and spatter his paint (in panels of the forties), a rhythmic technique which may have influenced the creation of Jackson Pollock's grandiose canvases. In these drip paintings Hofmann proved it conceivable to by-pass cubist stricture of form and surrealist dictates of subject, and still be able to paint freely and spontaneously without sacrificing a sense of innate form. In *Fantasia* this formal sense is derived from the calligraphic white line which weaves between the complementary color stains, separating them and relating them as the picture demands. What at first glance appears chaotic is actually infused with a new and personal sense of order.

As Hofmann advanced in age, his sense of formal order became ever more important. In the early fifties he began to use squares and rectangles in his compositions, and eventually these squared geometric shapes became his primary, though not his dominant, form. Hofmann's dominant "form" was always color, and for this reason the rather neutral shape of the rectangle appealed to him greatly. Even in highly ro-

mantic, free-flowing, expressionist paintings of his maturity, such as *Summer Night's Bliss,* the square form is still present. In this marvelous picture the square is the glowing center of the painting, active both in depth and on the surface. The orange square is the very core of the warm and sensuously harmonious composition, evoking the bliss of a summer night.

Peter Selz

109 FANTASIA 1943
Oil and duco on plywood; 51 1/2 x 36 1/2 inches
Dated and signed lower right:
43/ hans hofmann
Also dated and signed on back
Lent by the University Art Museum
University of California, Berkeley

110   SUMMER NIGHT'S BLISS   1961
Oil on canvas; 84 x 78 inches
Signed and dated lower right: *hans hofmann 61*
Inscribed, dated and signed on back:
Cat. 1294/ Summer Night's Bliss/
oil on canvas/ 1961/ 84 x 78/ Hans Hofmann
The Baltimore Museum of Art
Gift of the Artist

Edward Hopper
American, 1882-1967

111 TRAMP STEAMER 1908
Oil on canvas; 20 x 29 inches
Signed lower right: *E. HOPPER*
Lent from the Joseph H. Hirshhorn Collection

Edward Hopper seems a simple uncomplicated artist, easily understood, instantly grasped, manifestly rational. There are no optical enigmas in his paintings, no formal ambiguities to disturb the unity of his homely vision.

We think of Hopper as a distinctly American artist, even when national aesthetic boundaries have almost disappeared. We might say Hopper is American, because it is difficult to imagine his subject and style as having developed and matured anywhere else. He gives us an American experience rooted in the specifically American environment of the very recent past.

His aesthetic insularity evolved despite three visits to Europe between 1906 and 1910 when, like Eakins before him, he seems to have been untouched by the revolution that was sweeping away the principal concepts of art as they had been expounded by his teacher Robert Henri.

Tramp Steamer reveals the basic grammar of Hopper's artistic vocabulary. Although it is broadly painted, with traces of the Henri

swagger to remind us that he was a youthful contemporary of "The Eight," it is clearly painted in a manner too personal to be confused with the Henri group. The shapes are deliberately flattened, contrasts are sharpened, forms simplified, color localized and the space contracted. It is straight reportage, rejecting the romantic effects one associates with the subject, and it has the tough matter of fact look which anticipates the mature Hopper.

City Sunlight was painted forty-six years later. The shapes are even more deliberate, the brush severely restrained, every element is simplified and reduced to essentials. Formal pictorial concepts coexist with factual description. The windows in the painting recall the effect of a Mondrian, and our modern vision, attuned to such formal categorization, seeks to establish an affinity where none exists. Every element in the room has been similarly compacted, and this simplification of form is the only real tie Hopper has to modern formalist art.

But the value of Hopper's art exists beneath the apparent meaning it projects so simply. A more careful look reveals a puritanical denial of every sensuous pleasure paint allows. His one persistent device divides the world into light and shadow; the light, strong and pitiless, casts the shadows that are the dramatic agents of his paintings. This polarity of light and dark evokes subjective overtones of good and evil, life and death, allusive contrasts and contradictions. Although Hopper never uses the irrational images of the surrealist lexicon, his art is the closest expression we have to an American suprarealism in which he evokes the same feeling of isolation and timelessness we find in de Chirico, transferred from the desolate piazzas of Rome and Florence to the deserted thoroughfares of our Main Streets. His paintings are technically free from the detailed and clever rendering we find in magic realism, photographic realism or the other forms of realism which are evocative and melancholy.

His people are as impersonal as the objects which surround them. They live passively and isolated in an environment devoid of human warmth or empathy. In *City Sunlight* the woman's loneliness is felt as a physical pressure, real but mystifying. What does she wait for? Where Hopper's early contemporaries exploited the city as theater and its people as performers, Hopper is interested in its melancholy, anonymity and solitude. He senses its overwhelming power to isolate its inhabitants, all of whom are as unknown, alone and despondent as the rooms and streets they accidently inhabit.

Abram Lerner

112 CITY SUNLIGHT 1954
Oil on canvas; 28 x 40 inches
Signed lower right: *E. HOPPER*
Lent by the Joseph H. Hirshhorn Foundation

Vasily Kandinsky
Russian, 1866-1944

Few painters have sustained as relentless a stylistic continuity as did Vasily Kandinsky whose creative progression is rightly cited as a textbook example of evolutionary logic. From his post-impressionist and art nouveau beginnings in the opening years of this century, he moves first toward a figurative and then, gradually, toward an abstract expressionism that reaches its consummation at the outbreak of World War I. In a subsequent transitional phase his forms tighten and his imagery becomes more objective until, in twelve prolific Bauhaus years, something like an analogy to a musical grammar — a *Harmonielehre* — evolves through his painting and in his writings. After the rise of Nazism and the destruction of the Bauhaus, Kandinsky's eleven-year retreat to Paris produces a synthesis in which the insights gained in a striving life are projected within a new and moving context.

The distance which Kandinsky traveled is clearly indicated by the two examples placed here in juxtaposition — one marking his still tentative beginnings, the other an example of the summarizing capacities of his old age. *Amsterdam No. 52* may perhaps be designated as Kandinsky's earliest, fully successful painting. It was probably completed in 1904 when the artist was visiting this Dutch city, eight years after he had first submitted to formal art training upon his arrival in Munich from Russia. There are no extant examples from Kandinsky's hand before 1901, and *Amsterdam* stands out among early essays through the clarity and the crispness of its pictorial concept and through the relaxed bravura of its execution. Dotting his subject matter upon the surface, much as Pissarro did in his cityscapes of the 1890's, and tightening his intensively colored shapes, not unlike Munch at the turn of the century, Kandinsky firmly structures the small gem-like canvas to foretell through it the approaching fauvist phase of the Murnau years.

113 AMSTERDAM NO. 52 1904
Oil on board; 9 3/8 x 13 1/8 inches
Signed lower right: *KANDINSKY*
Lent by The Solomon R. Guggenheim Museum

Descriptive subject matter had vanished from Kandinsky's works long before he painted *Coolness,* which contains no traces of his figurative style. Nor is it, on the other hand, a formal exercise like some of the more arid Bauhaus canvases in which content seems to have evaporated with the elimination of the last vestiges of an observed reality. Thoroughly aware of the expressive potentialities of non-objective forms, Kandinsky, in such examples as this, enriches the potency of his vocabulary through associative references, succeeding thereby in the evocation of a world made of things rather than of ideas. The separate, emblematic form-images combine memories of an observed world with a grammatical exploration of the picture surface. "Concrete," as Kandinsky would have it, they obliterate the dichotomy between reality and abstraction.

Thomas M. Messer

114 COOLNESS 1941
Oil and lacquer on cardboard
19 1/4 x 27 5/8 inches
Monogrammed and dated lower left: *VK 41*
Lent by Mr. and Mrs. David Lloyd Kreeger

Ernst Ludwig Kirchner

German, 1880-1938

115 FLOWER BEDS IN THE
DRESDEN GARDENS   c.1910
Oil on canvas; 30 1/2 x 37 1/4 inches
The Baltimore Museum of Art
Gift of Curt Valentin Gallery, Inc.

The creative attitudes expressed in Kirchner's writings help to introduce us to the nature and direction of his painting development. For Kirchner art was a fusion of "the conscious" with "feeling," of discipline and craft with imagination and invention (1927). He rejected outright any photographic faithfulness to nature, yet he wished to present contemporary life in pictorial form: of necessity his search was therefore for a universally intelligible "art in a language of symbolic form" (1937). One aspect of Kirchner's solution was a particularly important one, found first in woodcuts and drawings: "hieroglyphs [which] convey the forms of nature in more simplified planear forms" (1920). In both *Flower Beds in the Dresden Gardens* and *Mountain Forest*, the arbitrarily triangular tree shapes and the architectonic, strongly simplified linear design represent such hieroglyphs. The fascinating play between space and surface, nature and decorative principle, languid summer silence and compellingly evocative color, all comprise Kirchner's language of symbolic form. Both landscapes confirm the

artist's lifelong commitment to an art embracing life and nature, as experienced through subjective vision. They are expressively direct and formally concise.

Kirchner was almost always able to keep representational challenge, expressional immediacy and decorative logic in a controlled balance. This is Kirchner's primary contribution to modern painting. Like Matisse and Klee, he found personal solutions to the general problems of the subjectivist creative process first posed in the post-impressionist generation. He also remained committed to the specifically *synthétiste* viewpoint whereby art comprises an important bridge between the only two poles given modern man: self and world. In this way, too, questioning in 1925 the value of non-objective art on principle, he remained with Matisse and Klee at the vital center of the early modern tradition.

Yet the differences between the two paintings, separated by a time span of nearly two decades, indicate Kirchner's development. *Dresden Gardens* was created by a painter who, shortly before, had welcomed any

138

116 MOUNTAIN FOREST
(Forest Path in Summer) 1927-28
Oil on canvas; 53 x 39 inches
Signed and inscribed on back:
E. L. Kirchner, Wildboden Bergwald
Lent by the University of Nebraska
F. M. Hall Collection

artist "who renders immediately and genuinely that which drives him to create" (1906). It is the work of an artist familiar with paintings by van Gogh, Munch and Matisse, who would soon expand the primitivism of Gauguin to encompass African, Oceanic, Buddhist Indian, and other expressive and sensuous art forms. *Dresden Gardens* is distinguished by a spontaneity of execution (the canvas has been left untouched in small areas) and possesses a vibrancy of color that has been retained despite minor color alterations made a decade later by the artist. Kirchner sees it as more typical of his "work from ocular experiences in the field of vision," while *Mountain Forest* represents his "independent work born in the imagination" (1927). The style of the later painting has the art of coptic tapestries for analogue, and is both more abstract and more decoratively sophisticated than the earlier one. It is more remote, cooler in tonality, yet has a monumentality and timelessness which is wholly appropriate to the lonely grandeur of alpine Switzerland. Less immediate perhaps, the later work speaks Kirchner's personal language at a more deeply imaginative level.

Donald E. Gordon

Paul Klee

Swiss (German School), 1879-1940

117 A HOTEL 1913
Watercolor; 9 1/4 x 8 1/4 inches
Signed upper right: *Klee*
Dated and inscribed lower left:
1913 120 Ein Hotel
The Baltimore Museum of Art
Nelson and Juanita Greif Gutman Collection

To anyone who thinks an artist's style progresses step by step from one phase to another, Paul Klee's work must seem a bewildering and confounding exception to the norm. One might well question whether Klee ever developed a style at all in the usual sense of the word. At certain times he did exhibit a preference for particular signs and symbols, particular qualities of line and tone and particular relationships among them. One can, as a matter of fact, recognize his "handwriting." But the development of style seems to imply a systematic borrowing from oneself and, though Klee did borrow from himself, he was scarcely systematic about it. Each picture or group of pictures presented a unique problem and therefore necessitated the creation of a unique solution.

The two works exhibited demonstrate clearly that there is no necessary and inevitable relationship between date and style. *A Hotel,* painted in 1913, might just as well have been done in 1923 or even in 1933; and the *Traveling Circus* of 1937, with its free relationship of forms and pointillist execution, contrasts sharply with *Superchess* (Grohmann, n.d., p. 292) of the same year, which is rigid and regular in its rectilinear order, smooth and dense in its painted surfaces. This is not to say that there is no development at all, but it does suggest that the study of Klee's development and hence the investigation of his early and late styles is likely to be less fruitful than is the case with many other artists, though the two works shown do suggest some of Klee's interests at the beginning and the end of his career.

In *A Hotel,* Klee, characteristically peering beyond the surface, reduces the world to geometry, dissecting the surface plane into relatively discrete units and unifying it by repetition and *passage.* The interplay of lines and planes recalls cubist practice and reminds one that Klee had gone to Paris and familiarized himself with French cubism in 1912. The character of the shapes, however, is less reminiscent of Picasso and Braque than of Delaunay, whom Klee had

140

visited on his trip and whose essay on light he had translated for *Der Sturm*. Abstracted though it is, the picture seems relatively conservative, an image of the world seen through the eye rather than discovered in the form or projected from the mind, as so much of Klee's imagery had been and would be. But the manner in which the shapes tumble about the surface in broken rhythms, the insistent contrast of straight line and curve, and the repetition of ellipses, lozenges and hourglass figures will be recurrent in his composition to the end.

In the late thirties the miniaturism that had characterized so much of his work gave way to a more expansive approach, even though older methods were still respected: forms and format became larger, lines more band-like, color more intense and spectral, and compositions looser, freer, more open. There was a tendency, also, to utilize more drastically abbreviated signs. *Traveling Circus*, in which the equipment and the composition itself are as acrobatic as the performers, is suggestive of his development at the end, though the compactness of the shapes, the continuity of the line and the abstract pointillism which decorates the planes exhibit much less freedom in conception and execution than other works of Klee's last years.

Lincoln Johnson

118 TRAVELING CIRCUS 1937
Oil on canvas; 25 1/2 x 19 3/4 inches
Dated on stretcher: *1937*
The Baltimore Museum of Art
Saidie A. May Collection

Franz Kline
American, 1910-62

"Hell, half the world wants to be like Thoreau at Walden worrying about the noise of traffic on the way to Boston; the other half use up their lives being part of that noise. I like the second half. Right?"

As much as any other artist of his generation, Franz Kline infused in his paintings his acceptance and admiration of the mechanical and societal power peculiar to American life. Born in eastern Pennsylvania where coal and railroad industries thrived, Kline from the beginning was exposed to the industrial giantism which has so strongly shaped the American scene. After his formal art training in Boston and London was completed, he most appropriately settled in 1938 in New York, the city which stands as a living definition for the extraordinary energy, monumentality, accomplishments and accompanying problems of American society.

The great achievement of such artists as Kline and Jackson Pollock was their painstaking development of singularly personal abstract styles which incorporated simultaneously the expressive potentialities of their immediate world and their individual qualities as artists and human beings. During the 1940's, in such paintings as *Chatham Square,* Kline worked in a semi-realistic manner which, affected by Cézanne and ultimately cubist ideas, still evinced his concern for developing illusionistic space and defining visible form. However, elements of his later abstract style are already present. Kline, who painted such scenes in his studio away from the actual location, has emphasized the movement of strong lines which form a structure across the surface of the picture, bringing to mind the linear black patterns of his subsequent work.

The key to Kline's ultimate liberation from realistic subject matter lay in the hundreds of investigatory drawings made during this decade of self-discovery. A matter of happenstance brought the stylistic content of his sketches to the threshold of his new style. As Elaine De Kooning relates (1962, pp. 14-15), "One day in 1949, Kline dropped in on a friend who was enlarging some of his own small sketches in a Bell-Opticon. 'Do you have any of those little drawings in your pocket?' the friend asked. Franz always did and supplied a handful. Both he and his friend were astonished at the change of scale and dimension . . . A four by five inch brush drawing of the rocking chair *.* . . loomed in gigantic black strokes expanding as entities in themselves, unrelated to any reality but that of their own existence . . .

119 CHATHAM SQUARE 1948
Oil on canvas; 40 x 30 inches
Signed lower right: *Franz Kline*
Lent by Mr. and Mrs. I. David Orr

120 PALLADIO 1961
Oil on canvas; 104 1/2 x 76 inches
Lent by the Joseph H. Hirshhorn Foundation

From that day, Franz Kline's style of painting changed completely."

Now came the struggle with monumental canvases which necessitated the use of new materials — liquid oil and enamel paints and large house painters' brushes. Since his new style developed directly from his previous drawings rather than his paintings, and since he wished to get to the essentials of a direct, gestural painting method which would convey with immediate impact the generalized message of his abstract forms, Kline eliminated color from his work. He continued to develop pictorial ideas in drawings, sometimes transferring them intact to his paintings, and at other times altering them extensively during the painting process. One of Kline's major artistic challenges was to maintain in his carefully worked paintings the immediacy and directness of handwriting present in his drawings. He strove to combine in his paintings the positive qualities of both gestural action and conscious control. However, the major problem which he posed for himself was the massing and bringing into balance of huge surface areas of black and white so that neither dominated the other. The tension which he created by forcing the viewer to read the white areas as positive shapes and not as background for the black images contributes substantially to the almost brutal dynamic energy which his paintings generate.

Once Kline found the style through which he could express himself most directly, he remained remarkably consistent. In some paintings he broke from his adherence to constructing separated areas of sharp blacks and whites and created instead tumultuous canvases filled with tonal gradations of gray, black and a variety of tinted blacks. From the mid-fifties on he even began to employ color again in some of his paintings. Nevertheless, in such late works as *Palladio,* he was still attacking the same problems that beset him upon viewing his drawings enlarged upon a studio wall that day in 1949.

Elaine De Kooning in her introduction to the catalogue of the Kline Memorial Exhibition wrote: "Kline carried on his private investigation of his non verbal thoughts . . . attempting to fulfill his endless urge to comment, to analyze, to deduce, to combine, to act out — and finally — to amaze, to offer something brand-new. 'Art has nothing to do with knowing,' Franz said. 'It has to do with giving' " (1962, p. 14).

Diana F. Johnson

Fernand Léger
French, 1881-1955

Unlike the cubists with whom he is traditionally associated, Léger never submitted to a period of rigorous discipline in choice of subject, limited color, depth, and minute fragmentation of forms. He rarely painted still lifes and never had a period that can be called "analytical" in the sense that this term is descriptive of Picasso and Braque through 1912. Instead, Léger, from the beginning of his career, was interested in particularly robust subjects, themes with social and popular overtones, clearly indicative of interests that the artist consistently pursued over the long course of his artistic career. *The Smokers* shows Léger investing a more traditional genre subject with new vitality. One generally thinks of "smokers" as a theme in Dutch seventeenth-century painting; here it is made relevant to twentieth-century life by the fusion of the subject, hearty village types — workers — into the context of modern industrial society. Their town, its trees, the smoke from chimneys, even clouds, become a pattern of interlocking metaphors describing modern man's life in a composition that is vibrant, bold and tough. Fragmentation and distortion are developed in order to present a full and complex range of meaning, any part of which, treated alone, would not have been true to the conditions of life. Léger perceived their reality as simultaneous, interlocking and definitely not evocative of old-fashioned sentiment, hence impossible to be captured by simple description. *The Smokers* is already the definitive Léger.

Léger's formal vocabulary from 1911 to the end of his career naturally underwent significant changes, but these can best be understood in terms of the relative consistency of his intentions with regard to meaning, allowing also for general stylistic shifts that took place in French painting from cubism through the Second World War. From the beginning, and *The Smokers* is a superb illustration, he favored the bold delineation of simple shapes. In the first period, prior to 1914, he emphasized volume with strong chiaroscuro. Dark and light shading, to stress powerful volumes, was so emphatic as to form an almost detachable set of patterns. In the late paintings, such as *Two Acrobats and Three Birds*, a vigorous line describes the simple shapes, and the role, once fulfilled by patterns of dark and light shading, is assumed by apparently independent color swathes which cut across the linear forms. In both his early and his late manner the composition is a result of cubist structure which violates appearances for the sake of presenting the

121 THE SMOKERS 1911
Oil on canvas; 50 x 38 1/2 inches
Lent by The Solomon R. Guggenheim Museum

144

122 TWO ACROBATS AND THREE BIRDS 1953
Oil on canvas; 23 3/8 x 36 inches
Signed and dated lower right: *F. LEGER . 53*
Lent by Mr. and Mrs. Charles Zadok

essentials of a more complex reality, generally limited to subjects of the city, machines, and urban enjoyment of the country and of popular spectacles.

Actually, Léger's range of thematic ideas was not very great. He was not a prodigious inventor of meaning like Picasso; instead, like a good Norman peasant, he never wasted an idea. Every subject and every formal invention was put to good use, sometimes even twenty and thirty years after its initial use. No part of Léger's career exemplifies this so well as the great series of interrelated works he produced during the last fifteen years of his life. One of the themes, the circus, culminates in the *Great Parade* of 1954 (Guggenheim Museum); and one of the major canvases that fits into the development of the *Great Parade* is the *Two Acrobats and Three Birds*. Léger's interest in acrobats went back at least twenty-five years, and their placement alongside the circle of the circus ring had developed in connection with other studies for the *Great*

Parade. The inclusion of the birds recalls not only the circus context, but especially another major Léger theme, *The Country Outing,* where men and women — always city dwellers — taste the pleasures of the country. His city people, like the circus performers or the construction gangs, are types for whom Léger had profound admiration. If elements from *Two Acrobats,* such as the circus ring, recall the bicycle wheel or the automobile wheel from other paintings, or if the pattern of rectangles along the bottom of the ring suggests the girders from *The Constructors* and then turns into a tree branch, it is because Léger's final paintings are interrelated in their ultimate meaning which is essentially a celebration of the common man. His common man, from *The Smokers* of 1911 to the *Two Acrobats* of 1953, is a being whose life is pervaded by the industrial age he has created, but who has never lost his joy in nature and art.

Daniel Robbins

145

John Marin
American, 1870-1953

123 EAST RIVER 1910
Watercolor; 12 1/2 x 16 inches
Signed and dated lower right: *Marin/ 10*
Lent from the Collection of
Edith Gregor Halpert

John Marin was a water-colorist all his life. The early Marin is a gentle, somewhat tentative artist, both in his drawing and in his application of color. A wobbly and even illustrational quality comes through, although the fine freedom of the washed brush strokes is an indication of the more forceful and defined Marin of the next decade. In the early *East River* the water tilts back to a clearly marked horizon line, the always recognizable skyline of lower Manhattan which rises to establish a wall over which the sky and sun arch toward us. The resulting vignette is both traditional and advanced; the spatial relationships and the planes and the notational system are reminiscent of earlier water colors; the dislocation of form and color, the casually washed color are newer and less expected.

Four decades later, in *The Tempest*, the water is the ocean, the notations are firmer and more abstract, the horizon line is higher, and most notable of all, the water lies flat against the picture plane. This effect is heightened by the frame within the frame, the rock-like forms that do not touch the edges of the paper. As in contemporary works by Jackson Pollock, the abstract rhythms are contained and made non-arbitrary by the ways in which they return upon themselves and never trail off at the edges.

The few Feininger-like lines in the sky date the artist as one who knew the cubists and the futurists in his formative years. The freedom of execution, the heightened color and the forceful abstract rhythms of *The Tempest* indicate why John Marin has continued to interest us through the change in taste occasioned by abstract expressionism.

Henry Geldzahler

124 THE TEMPEST 1952
Watercolor; 14 1/2 x 19 inches
Signed and dated lower right: *Marin 52*
Lent by the Joseph H. Hirshhorn Foundation

Henri Matisse
French, 1869-1954

125   THE BLUE NUDE (Souvenir de Biskra)   1907
Oil on canvas; 36 1/4 x 55 1/8 inches
Signed lower right: *Henri Matisse*
The Baltimore Museum of Art
Cone Collection

In 1948, at the time of his large retrospective exhibition in Philadelphia, Henri Matisse summarized his artistic goals with eloquent simplicity: "I have always tried to hide my own efforts and wished my works to have the lightness and joyousness of a springtime which never lets anyone suspect the labors it has cost." By the time that observation was made, late in life, the justice of its metaphor had already been confirmed by actual accomplishment. Matisse managed to sustain those ideals for the brief but productive years that were left to him before his death in 1954. Many other modern artists had, of course, similarly reconciled the complexities born of youthful exploration with the simpler, purer forms they evolved in later life. Kandinsky, Klee and Mondrian, for example, here come

to mind. But the simplifications cultivated by Matisse possess a seemingly artless innocence that makes his seasonal allusion peculiarly apt. It is as though he had found some secret power of creative rejuvenation which finally enabled him to compress the findings of a lifetime into the bud of perpetual promise. The two late works in the present exhibition illustrate that side of Matisse's art. A third, the early *Blue Nude*, represents the decades of patient, almost relentless effort which had prepared the way for that eventual release, and which alone would justify the pre-eminence of Matisse among the masters of twentieth-century art.

Matisse painted *The Blue Nude* early in 1907. The subtitle of the canvas, "souvenir of Biskra," refers to the palm leaves in the landscape background, included in reminiscence of the artist's visit to Algeria the previous year. In a sense, the figure is a free variation on the familiar *Salon* subject of the female nude. Like Delacroix, Ingres, Renoir and Gauguin before him, Matisse would in future years find special attraction in the feminine form seen against a luxuriant setting or clad in exotic costume. But at this point in his career, Matisse was not inclined to exploit the more obvious charms of those subjects, as he would later do in his *odalisques* of the 1920's and 1930's. Instead, he denied conventional notions of beauty in favor of a relatively abstract emphasis on salient shapes and resonant hues. As in a number of his earlier figure pieces, the color chords are based on blue. But the figure is here enlarged to life-size and the harmonies scaled to more active contrasts in the liberal introduction of pinks, violets, ochres and greens.

Matisse was hardly an inexperienced youth at the time he painted *The Blue Nude*. He was already approaching forty, but his reputation as a leader of the avant-garde was still quite new and highly controversial. The blazing colors and summary forms of the works he and his comrades had shown at the *Salon d'Automne* of 1905 had been widely dismissed as brutal or as "fauve." The extent to which the newcomers were following paths initiated by Cézanne, Gauguin, van Gogh and the neo-impressionists gained their art little popular credence. Those older masters themselves still remained suspect in the eyes of most critics. Undeterred by rejection, Matisse pressed further in his departures from accustomed standards. In 1906, his *Joy of Life* caused a scandal as a patent distortion of natural order. Today, it may be admired for an inventiveness of color and exuberance of form that are reiterated in *The Blue Nude*. Fauve usage is continued in the surprising juxtapositions of color and linear accent in both paintings. Yet there are signs of redirection of effort in the later canvas, particularly in its evidence of a renewed interest in the art of Cézanne. However arbitrary its elisions of space and form may be, both color and line reveal a more affirmatively plastic intent than is to be inferred from the decorative massing of color and the art nouveau sinuosity of line in the *Joy of Life*. To some extent, that new balance of elements may reflect the fact that Matisse was in *The Blue Nude* reworking a subject he had previously treated in sculpture. On the other hand, the painter's ventures from time to time into a three-dimensional medium indicate preoccupations with dynamic, substantial relationships of form, which are not fully accountable within the prior context of fauvism. Especially in the decade to follow the painting of *The Blue Nude*, a search for plastic redefinition — even occasional flirtations with cubism — strongly marked the course of Matisse's artistic development.

In the period between the two World Wars, Matisse consolidated the results of his prolonged involvement with new modes. The contrapuntal tensions of his earlier expression were at last resolved in an art of disarming concordance. In 1941 he underwent a grave operation. But advanced age and impaired health led to an amazing creative renewal, not to the retirement that might well have been expected. Aside from a number of major paintings, there was an impressive array of illustrations, tapestry cartoons and decorative projects for the chapel Matisse sponsored at Vence, all attesting to the vitality and range of his continued activity.

Interior with Egyptian Curtain is perhaps the most famous of the numerous interiors Matisse painted in the studio he maintained at Vence from 1944 to 1949. Its daring concept and freshness of execution confound the viewer's awareness that its maker was then in his eightieth year. New meanings have been uncovered in a theme he had approached often before, particularly in his use of black as an active component of the color structure. Even more than in the many early compositions in which black is prominent, that normally neutral tone takes on the quality of coloristic brilliance in its function as a foil to the contrasting hues against which it has been set — the glowing foliage and sky seen through the window and the adjacent hanging with its brash pattern. And the black shadow cast by the fruit bowl assumes much the same properties of intensity as the blues that often occur in comparable passages in Matisse's still lifes of an earlier era. The arresting impact of the color is borne out in a counterplay of shapes which would be unruly, but for the master's grasp of the larger design relationships and his ability to balance one compelling visual force with another. The total result is one of bursting vigor, in place of the mellow richness that had generally characterized Matisse's works of the middle years.

For what proved to be his last works, Matisse turned from easel painting to the medium of gouache and cut paper. In part, the technique of using *papiers découpés*

126   INTERIOR WITH EGYPTIAN CURTAIN   1948
Oil on canvas; 45 1/2 x 35 inches
Signed and dated lower right: *Matisse 48*
Lent from The Phillips Collection

had been adopted out of practical considerations. It permitted the subtlest readjustments of design without loss of the effect of spontaneity and enabled the ailing master to continue his work, even though he was confined to his bed. Fortunately the new medium also proved to be admirably suited to his aesthetic intentions for such projects as the designing of stained glass and liturgical artifacts for the chapel at Vence and the rendition of working drawings from which color lithographs, including the *Jazz* series, could be made. A number of large, independent compositions were executed by the same process. *Fleurs de Neige* exemplifies the joyous brilliance of the group as a whole. In their enlarged form, the *papiers découpés* recapture the wholesome freedom of the early decorative works, such as *The Dance*. Their niceties of design convey the spirit of adult play, not academic exercise. No more fitting after-image of a lifetime inspired by the affirmative promise of spring could be imagined than the generous scatter of blossoming forms Matisse has so vivaciously arranged against their colorful trellis.

Frank Andersen Trapp

127   FLEURS DE NEIGE   1951
Gouache on cut and pasted paper
68 1/8 x 32 inches
Inscribed, signed and dated lower right:
Fleurs de Neige Henri Matisse/ 1951
Lent by Mrs. Albert Sperry

Joan Miró
Spanish, 1893-

Superficially viewed, much of the work of Joan Miró appears disarming and naive, the spontaneous invention of a precocious *enfant terrible* who has commandeered his father's paints. Actually, of course, his work is the product of long, patient and rigorous training, of sophisticated speculation and of far-ranging knowledge of contemporary art. Often the early works seem to display the various current styles in separate parts of a picture and to become painted anthologies of early twentieth-century art. In *Spanish Farm Landscape* the manipulation of color values in the architecture recalls Cézanne; the preciseness, clarity and decorative quality in the details are reminiscent of Henri Rousseau; the bright tones of the distant landscape resemble those of Chagall, the German expressionists and the fauves; the transformations of nature in the sky approach Kandinsky; and the interrelation-

ships of forms point to the piquant perspectives and ambiguous spaces of cubism, now advancing, now retreating, now lying flat. Yet Miró never slavishly imitates. All the diverse reminiscences merge in an inseparable wholeness, submitting to the personality of the author, whose whole career seems devoted to unifying the most unlikely and contrasting material and to making the incompatible compatible.

Already in 1918 much of the later, more familiar Miró is apparent: the penchant for line, the astonishing combinations of descriptive representation, free form and geometric abstraction, the creation of frames within frames by the overlapping of motifs. During the next four years, inspired in part by his association with the dadaists and in part by his admiration for Matisse, Miró developed one of the most personal, provocative and innovative modes of the twentieth

128 SPANISH FARM LANDSCAPE
(The Tileworks at Montroig) 1918
Oil on canvas; 25 1/2 x 32 inches
Signed and dated lower left: *Miró/ 1918*
Lent by Mr. and Mrs. David Lloyd Kreeger

129 CHANTEUSE D'OPERA 1966
Oil on canvas; 31 3/4 x 21 1/4 inches
Lent by the Perls Galleries

century, transforming the anti-style of dada into style and creating images which, if they have the simplicity of Matisse, are far richer in metaphorical content. The picture plane became not an area to be composed but a space in which forms were freely suspended; line, tensile and sinuous, formed extraordinary associations with flat planes of color; and line, shape, color and texture acquired multivalent significance in their references to nature and to feelings.

In the years between 1918 and 1966, Miró also created a system of ideographic forms which he manipulated like moveable type. Combining and recombining the familiar shapes, he added overtones by varying the accent like a Japanese calligrapher; but always he preserved the reference to nature, however generalized it might be. Some of the characters appear in the *Chanteuse d'Opéra* of 1966: the concentric circles, the tic-tac-toe square, the undulating tendril, the oval blob.

Like Klee, Miró uses titles both as signposts to orient the spectator and as means of limiting imaginative flights. And like Klee, he uses words within his pictures and sometimes makes pictures out of words, as if to imply that the function of picture-making is not to create structures but to inspire feelings, and that for such a purpose words and forms have equivalent value and may work in harmony. The title *Chanteuse d'Opéra* thus becomes, more than a designation, part of the work. It is the verbal correlative of the thing, while the image is the visual correlative of feelings, movements and sounds. So the singer swells, postures and gesticulates, and the sounds become visible, vibrating in the picture space, breaking the sight barrier; and singer and song, comedy and beauty become one.

By this time Miró's style has become more painterly and freer than ever before. But, for all the patent differences from the earlier work, there are reminders of the unity in his oeuvre. Interestingly enough, the areas of color are given breathing spaces, an idea explored by the fauves, whom Miró had so much admired at the beginning of his career. And if one looks carefully at certain parts of the *Spanish Landscape*, one can see, already adumbrated, the basic patterns of the *Chanteuse d'Opéra* and, early or late, Miró's affirmation of the world about him. "For me a form is never abstract," he once said. "It is always a man, a bird or something else. For me painting is never form for form's sake."

Lincoln Johnson

Piet Mondrian
Dutch, 1872-1944

130 HORIZONTAL TREE 1911-12
Oil on canvas; 29 5/8 x 43 7/8 inches
Signed lower left: *MONDRIAN*
Lent by the Munson-Williams-Proctor Institute

Chronologically, *Horizontal Tree* and *Composition London* bracket in large measure the somewhat more than three decades throughout which Piet Mondrian employed one or another form of grid arrangement as a basic component of his major paintings. Before he arrived at this compositional solution, he experimented for a number of years in the Netherlands with a variety of naturalistic and, subsequently, pointillist-influenced styles. Indeed, a large preparatory charcoal drawing for *Horizontal Tree* in the collection of the Municipal Museum, The Hague (Blok, 1964, No. 120) derives chiefly from the former of these phases, since it is replete with descriptive detail and, furthermore, displays no accompanying grid. In contrast, the pervading network of vertical and horizontal line segments underlying the painting justifies readjusting its traditional 1911 dating to the following year, when Mondrian first worked in Paris and developed this form of grid from the cubism originating there. Two very slightly later oil

versions of this subject (Blok, 1964, Nos. 121 and 122) also employ such a grid, albeit embedded more deeply in the painting surface, and the 1912 date of these works is generally acknowledged. All three painted versions of this theme manifest a spirit foreign to that of orthodox French cubism through their use of involuted elliptical contours in the vitalistic rendering of the central tree motif.

If *Horizontal Tree* betrays a certain monochromatic bias close to that of cubism in its thinly applied grayish coloration, it also bears traces of bright spectral hues which must be considered inspired vestiges of the artist's previous experience in the Netherlands. In this and other transitional paintings, Mondrian has disciplined into a singular aesthetic coherence a veritable maelstrom of such polar opposites as linear vs. planear, straight vs. curved, color vs. tonality, static vs. dynamic.

Apart from the exclusion of curved lines, *Composition London* is also based upon juxtaposed polarities of basic plastic elements, although they are here realized in radically purified form. It was perhaps the last finished painting begun in 1940 by Mondrian while he was still in Europe, although, like numerous other paintings from the late 1930's, it was completed only in 1942 (for an exhibition in New York City) presumably by adding certain lines and color planes to intensify the dynamics of rhythm in accordance with the more complex syncopations of his ultimate "Boogie Woogie" phase. In fact, through a generic similarity to several other drawings and canvases which apparently were begun about 1939-40 in London but left unfinished at his death in 1944 (Seuphor, 1956, p. 394, Ills. 431, 432 and 434) *Composition London* constitutes a guide to Mondrian's immediate pre-New York activity. This is particularly true, if one eliminates in one's mind the most obvious new world additions of small unenclosed color areas along the left edge of the painting. *Composition London* uses lines of more uniform width, more even spacing and shows a greater tendency to enclose the areas of white ground than do those compositions known to have originated at a somewhat earlier date. Thus, this pivotal late work and the early *Horizontal Tree* illustrate how Mondrian's pictorial language evolved as much in response to the laws of inner change as to the stimulus of the styles and physical environments encountered successively in Paris and New York.

Robert P. Welsh

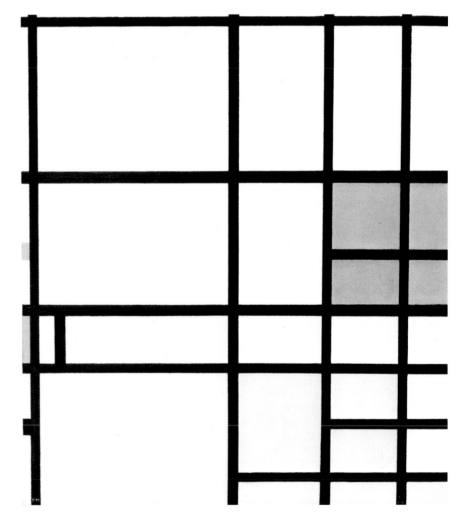

131 COMPOSITION LONDON 1940-42
Oil on canvas; 32 1/2 x 28 inches
Initialed lower left: *P M*
Dated lower right: *40/ 42*
Lent by the Albright-Knox Art Gallery

Pablo Picasso

Spanish, 1881-

Certainly no artist of Picasso's stature, and possibly no artist in history, has in his work so extensively and profoundly illustrated, examined, probed and analyzed the nature of his own creative activity, the character of the man as artist, the relationship between the artist and his subject and even, at times, the implications of his work for his own life and for the history of art. Picasso's use of art as a theme manifests itself as well in the quantity of works in which the art of other masters is his subject matter and Picasso a kind of critic in paint.

He develops the theme in every phase of his career, sometimes with symbolist indirection, as when he paints himself as Harlequin seated at a bar (1903); sometimes directly, as in a self portrait with palette (1906); sometimes analytically, as in the series of etchings, *The Sculptor's Studio* (1937) or in the drawings assembled for publication under the title *The Human Comedy* (1953). And there are other, less overt references as well. The number in-

creases as the cubist and surrealist struggles to redefine art recede into history and as Picasso's works become, more and more, fragments of a painted autobiography.

An even more persistent theme has been woman. His brush has represented her visual appearance, caressed her seductive but constantly escaping forms, x-rayed her, dissected her, and deified her, analyzed her as object and psychoanalyzed her as *persona*, treated her to tender sympathy, observed her with ironic criticism and submitted her to animal attack.

The two themes, art and woman, coalesce in *The Painter and His Model in the Garden*, painted on 5-6 May, 1963, one of a series of related works executed from February through July of that year. In its style the picture suggests how not only themes but methods and manners may fuse; for in *The Painter and His Model* preoccupations of earlier modes—once developed deliberately, now used automatically—are synthesized in an almost magical *tour de force*.

132 WOMAN WITH BANGS 1902
Oil on canvas; 23 5/8 x 19 1/4 inches
Signed upper left: *Picasso*
The Baltimore Museum of Art
Cone Collection

133 NUDE 1909
Oil on canvas; 36 1/2 x 24 3/4 inches
Signed lower left: *Picasso*
Lent from the Collection of
Dr. and Mrs. Israel Rosen

Some of the principal features of earlier manners are illustrated in the other works in this exhibition. *Woman with Bangs* (1902) is symptomatic not only of Picasso's originality but of his awareness of art historical developments in the period. Its simplified, sculpturesque volumes, its combinations of volume and plane, and its clean, hard contours are reminiscent of Gauguin and the primitives; its curvilinear structures vaguely echo art nouveau, against which, with rectilinear vengeance, Picasso was later to rebel; and its almost monochromatic blue suggests the symbolist preoccupation with *l'azur,* whether in poetry, as in Mallarmé, or in painting, as in Maurice Denis and Isidro Nonell. For all the overt brushwork, the painting imposes an almost impenetrable density to the eye; but that hardness of style, coupled with a tenderness of sentiment, transforms pathos into a fundamental aspect of existence and characterizes much of Picasso's work at the time.

The *Nude* (1909) historically marks the transition from early Neo-Platonic or idealistic cubism to analytical or facet cubism. Idealistic cubism had exhibited the simple, regular volumes underlying geometrically complex organisms; facet cubism developed more complicated rhythms of form, created a more complete fusion of solid and void and injected the element of time into the static world of the painting, partly by representing objects from a variety of station points simultaneously — which implied the movement of the artist through space and hence through time — and partly by presenting the various views in such complete unity that their relationships in deep space become ambiguous, so that the viewer's perception of space changes in time. In the *Nude* the figure is still an independent entity, though the simplified planes that compose it melt into one another and vigorously thrust and withdraw in the picture space. The artist's interest in line and contour persists, as it will through most of his career, along with his deliberate departure from appearance and insistence on the significance of abstract form.

Woman Seated (1959) exhibits Picasso's penchant for architectonic structure and a persistent interest in volumes that is related to his excursions into sculpture. But more important, it suggests his tendency, more and more frequent in his later years, to combine cubist grammatical structure with a more naturalistic vocabulary, both in the forms represented and in the suggestions of light and shadow absent from so much of his earlier art. As in so many of his works, the various aspects of the picture carry varying overtones. The sadness and introspection of *Woman with Bangs* reappears in the head, with its Byzantine eyes so reminiscent of his wife's — or of his own when confronted with David Douglas Duncan's photograph of a dead marine. Yet the forms, angular and pointed, rounded and elongated, simultaneously pull away from and penetrate one another, exploding with energy. They also abound in pictorial witticisms, reminding us that Picasso, as much as anybody, has injected humor into "fine" art: the various anatomical parts are breast-like, phallic, cuneate and skeletal in their affinities; an ear pulls at the adjacent cheek; a rounded breast becomes angular, a nipple triangular; underarm moustaches splinter into radial patterns and strands of hair flay the space about them; the huge extended feet and the small shoes become amusing, not simply in their comparative scale but in the economic appropriateness of their shapes as well. Everywhere wit is reinforced by an apparent spontaneity and directness of execution. However, the tectonic organization of the picture as a whole and the restrained tonality are quite different, holding in check this overwhelming

134 WOMAN SEATED 1959
Oil on canvas; 57 1/2 x 45 inches
Signed upper left: *Picasso*
Dated on back:
14.2.59/ 18.2.59/ 19.22/ 8.-9.-3.59
Lent from the Collection of
Mr. and Mrs. Victor W. Ganz

135 THE PAINTER AND HIS MODEL
IN THE GARDEN 1963
Oil on canvas; 35 x 45 1/2 inches
Signed lower left: *Picasso*
Lent by the Perls Galleries

figure that threatens to burst from the picture plane and investing it with some of the monumental aloofness and austerity associated with the classical figures of thirty years earlier. Pathos and comedy, the particular and the general, energy and constraint fuse as they do in life itself and as they did more overtly in *The Human Comedy* six years earlier.

The Painter and His Model in the Garden continues, refines, elaborates and modifies the qualities apparent in the other works: the simplified forms and frank linearity of the blue period, the structural division of the picture plane and the interplay between surface pattern and deep space found in cubism, and the synthesis of geometry and naturalism seen in the *Woman Seated*. The bisecting of the canvas, still daring a century after Degas had begun to explore the idea, separates the world of the painter from the world of the model, as if to acknowledge the manifold differences between them. But the two areas are brought into a more positive relationship by a va-

riety of organizational means. (For example, with customary wit, Picasso suggests the bones of the painter's arm, fits one of them into the shape of the buttocks and the canvas seat of the stool, then picks up the motif on the other side of the picture.)

For all the reminiscences of earlier works, the method employed here is more painterly: the record of the brush's movement and even the plastic qualities of the paint itself suggest fluidity and freedom — and absolute control. Picasso has said of his work of this time that he has sought to find signs for things, not to represent the appearance of a breast but to find a shape that will say breast in much the same way a word does. In his aim, if not in his solution, he is thus like other twentieth-century artists — notably Klee and Miró — who have developed an ideographic syllabary of forms. He seems, in fact, almost to write his compositions and, to use his own imagery, to paint as the birds sing.

Lincoln Johnson

159

Jackson Pollock
American, 1912-56

Jackson Pollock's poured paintings distract us from other achievements in his mature career. His popular fame rests on technical innovations rather than on his evolution during the decade which begins with works such as *Pasiphaë* (1943) and ends with *Portrait and a Dream* (1953). Pollock's previous development from 1933 to 1943 is marked by a transition from the manner of Benton and Ryder to that of Picasso and Miró. This change coincides with a mental crisis in 1938 and his first meetings with the artist-critic John Graham. Similarly, his subsequent development follows the pattern of his experience. *Pasiphaë,* painted in the year of his first recognition, should not be searched for details of the lurid myth (the work was first called *Moby Dick*) but encountered as reflecting both a stylistic and psychic state. The free calligraphy, the forms and colors which mask and model, illustrate Pollock's adaptation of "psychic automatism," the fundamentals of which he learned, not from the surrealists who came to New York in the early forties, but from sources such as John Graham in the late thirties. *Pasiphaë's* central oval and flanking totems impose order on a chaotic field of

136 PASIPHAE 1943
Oil on canvas; 56 1/8 x 96 inches
Signed lower left: *Jackson/ Pollock*
Lent by the Marlborough-Gerson Gallery, Inc.
Collection of Lee Krasner Pollock

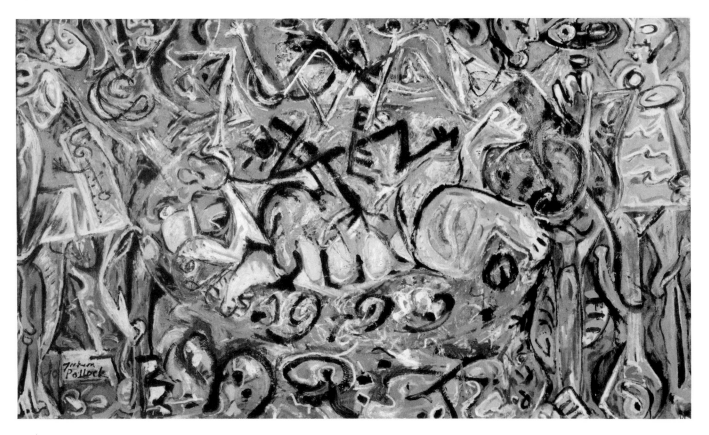

137 PORTRAIT AND A DREAM   1953
Enamel on canvas; 58 1/4 x 134 1/2 inches
Signed and dated lower right:
Jackson Pollock 53
Lent by the Dallas Museum of Fine Arts
Gift of Mr. and Mrs. Algur H. Meadows
and the Meadows Foundation

struggling detail. This configuration controls the content, implying on a deeper level, a personality aware but still unstabilized after a period of Jungian psychoanalysis. As such it can be seen as an abstraction of Pollock's search for personal integration which transcends, in myth, the title of the work.

Five years later, his alcoholism arrested, at the peak of his mental and physical health, Pollock no longer needed the control and symbolism of stable configurations but the greater freedom to gesture, to pour himself out in trajectories of color and silver whose arcs and rhythms, scaled to his total presence, fused art and the motion of life. Configuration and content became one in the process of painting. But this lasted only about two years.

The black and white paintings of 1951 and 1952 parallel renewed depression and drinking. *Portrait and a Dream,* painted in the last consistently productive year of his life, eschews the studied self-control of *Pasiphaë* and the confident self-abandon-

ment of the poured paintings for stark self-encounter. In the *Portrait and a Dream* early imagery recurs: the portrait-image (Pollock told a friend it depicted himself) is defined only on the right, thus echoing a similarly halved self portrait of 1938 on a page of sketches after El Greco. This half-masked face, painted in yellow, red and silver, co-exists on the same canvas with a typical black and white painting of the year before. The disparate configuration, set in the ambiguous space of dreams, mythologizes not the determined quest for unity found in *Pasiphaë* but the tense acceptance of the duality between art and self which marked the last three years of his life.

Pollock's power lies in the brutal fusion of his personality and art. With few other painters, from El Greco to now, is an understanding of the creator so needed for seeing the creation. But art so personal is also universal.

Francis V. O'Connor

Mark Tobey
American, 1890-

In the thirties at the time when Mark Tobey painted *Broadway,* there was a breakthrough of a new creative consciousness. With Jung interpreting the collective unconscious in the psychological field and Paul Klee evoking the subconscious force in his painting, a new era was born. Tobey sensed this in his own search to explore new fields and reinterpret old subjects. It is in this area that Tobey's work contributes so much.

Broadway was painted in Devonshire. In the quiet of an English countryside Tobey's impression of Broadway flowed from this inner creative urge until one almost hears the sounds and sees the lights and crowds that are the essence of Broadway. A painter no longer sits at his easel confronting his subject. He absorbs, digests and synthesizes this inner magic and tunes his creative energies to a high pitch. Furthermore, *Broadway* shows one of the early uses of his calligraphic technique which was later to become known as "white-writing."

The theme of cities, New York and Seattle in particular, is recurrent in Tobey's work, yet the western territory was also well known to him. Born in Wisconsin, he knew the plains, the desert towns, the ghost towns. Tobey's *Ghost Town,* painted in Switzerland, is alive with activity. Gnomelike faces peer out from the canvas, endless numbers are woven into the calligraphy. The density of the main street straggles along to diminish and fade into the outskirts. This town, perhaps once as alive as Broadway with miners and gamblers, lives on, if not in fact, at least in Tobey's vision. Here, the essence of another time and place in America is recorded from the same creative source as *Broadway.*

Tobey's art has many facets, moves in many directions, employs many ideas and is always inventive; each painting is completely different from all others. However, the entire body of his work is a steady development and refinement of his personal style.

Marian Willard Johnson

138 BROADWAY 1935-36
Tempera on masonite; 26 x 19 1/4 inches
Signed and dated lower right: *TOBEY/ 36*
Lent by The Metropolitan Museum of Art
Arthur H. Hearn Fund, 1942

139   GHOST TOWN   1965
Oil on canvas; 82 3/4 x 53 inches
Signed and dated lower right: *Tobey/ 65*
Lent by the Willard Gallery

Jacques Villon
French, 1875-1963

140 PORTRAIT OF THE PAINTER J. B. 1911
Oil on canvas; 50 3/4 x 35-inches
Signed and dated on back: *Jacques Villon 1911*
Lent by the Columbus Gallery of Fine Arts
Ferdinand Howald Collection

These two portraits by Jacques Villon are separated by forty years, yet it would be a good quiz question to ask which is later, for *Portrait of My Brother,* painted in 1951, is a recognizable portrait of Marcel Duchamp, while the *Portrait of the Painter J. B.* is an orphic mystery, which we would be at a loss to identify if Marcel Duchamp did not assure us that it represents Jacques Bon. We think of style in our time as proceeding from the representative to the abstract, and we expect abstraction to increase; in the case of Jacques Villon, it does not.

In analytical cubism modern art early attained a degree of abstraction which was later surpassed only by Malevich and, now, by the minimalists. In the case of the Duchamp family, both Jacques Villon and his brother Marcel soon attained such purity of concept and execution that they stopped painting.

Around 1911, when the *Portrait of J. B.* was painted, a number of artists used to meet at the Duchamp family studio. These artists, who were strongly influenced by the theories of Sérusier and Maurice Denis, were profoundly interested in numbers, proportion and the Golden Section; mathematics was magic, and proportion was Pythagorean. They thought that they had the ultimate secret of design and that even color could be reduced to a code. The painting theories that were so popular in the States in the twenties and so strongly influenced painters like George Bellows were pale reflections and reflexes of these activities. Seurat tried to find colors that would approximate natural light; these men used color as an end in itself. The group included Delaunay, Léger, Gleizes, Metzinger, Kupka and Picabia. Whereas Picasso and Braque started from the natural object and broke it up into planes, they started from the planes. Whereas Picasso and Braque simplified color to drab monotony, they used the entire spectrum. Compared to the *Portrait of J. B.*, an early cubist portrait is colorless and realistic.

Like his brother Marcel, for whom the veil of illusion dropped completely, Villon quit painting for a long time. When he returned to his art, he, like Delaunay and Gleizes, retreated to more realistic, more representative painting. From a theoretical point of view, this was a loss; from the point of view of painting, a gain. There is, in my judgment, no doubt that *Portrait of My Brother* is a far more penetrating, sensitive and perceptive work of art than *Portrait of J. B.* Here is the aging magician, the old philosopher, who has seen everything, and seen through everything, and kept nothing but his smile.

Mahonri Sharp Young

141 PORTRAIT OF MY BROTHER 1951
Oil on canvas; 31 7/8 x 23 3/4 inches
Signed and dated lower left: *Jacques Villon/ 51*
Inscribed, signed and dated on back:
Mon Frere Jacques Villon 1951
Lent by the Columbus Gallery of Fine Arts

Edouard Vuillard

French, 1868-1940

In a review of the *Salon d'Automne* of 1905 André Gide has interpreted with empathy the art of Vuillard, his contemporary: "I do not know what I like most here. Perhaps, M. Vuillard himself. I know few works where one is brought more directly into communion with the painter. This is due, I suspect, to his emotion never losing its hold on the brush . . . It is due to his speaking in a low tone, suitable to confidences, and to one's leaning over to listen to him . . . His melancholy is not romantic nor haughty, it is discreet and clothed in an everyday garment; it is caressingly tender, I might even say, timid, if this word were in consonance with such mastership. Yes, I see in him his success notwithstanding, the charm of anxiety and doubt. He never puts forward a colour without excusing it by some subtle and precious withdrawal, too modest to assert, he insinuates . . . No seeking for the showy, a constant search for harmony. By a grasp of relations, at once intuitive and studied, he explains each colour by its neighbor and obtains from both a reciprocal response . . ." (*Gazette des Beaux-Arts,* Dec. 1905, quoted in Roger-Marx, 1946, pp. 125-26).

Although Gide's comments were made in reference to a set of decorative panels which Vuillard had executed in 1896, they apply as well to his other early achievements and most particularly to his small easel paintings of the 1890's. As his friend and biographer, Roger-Marx (1946, p. 48) has pointed out: "At this period of his beginnings, he [Vuillard] incorporates the persons with the setting to such a degree that one gets the impression that by some law of mimesis, setting and person are one. A dress appears to be composed of the same material as the wall-paper. A profile seems to be woven. Wall-paper . . . takes on hallucinatory powers. The background wedges into the foreground . . . Objects nearly all of them, have more weight and more movement than the living . . ."

The canvas *Mother and Sister of the Artist* corresponds to this description of Vuillard's style in every respect but one: here the figure of Mme. Vuillard, monumentally conceived and strongly outlined, has been

142 MOTHER AND SISTER OF THE ARTIST c.1893
Oil on canvas; 18 1/4 x 22 1/4 inches
Signed lower right: *E. Vuillard*
Lent by The Museum of Modern Art, New York
Gift of Mrs. Saidie A. May

143 THE BEDROOM c.1920
Distemper on board; 27 x 29 1/2 inches
Signed lower right: *E. Vuillard*
The Baltimore Museum of Art
Frederic W. Cone Bequest

singled out and made the focal point — a composition that could be interpreted as a pictorial analogy to her role in the life and art of her son. These intimate little masterpieces — combining daring originality and quiet restraint, mystery and commonplace, geometric structure and overall pattern — brought Vuillard to the attention of the fashionable world of collectors and art dealers and established his early success; as a result of his rapidly growing reputation, he was offered many commissions to portray his flamboyant patrons in the sumptuous interiors of their homes. Did this new life affect the development of Vuillard's art? Within less than ten years, before he had reached the age of forty, his creativity decreased, his style became more detailed, more realistic, and much of his work lost its unique and enchanting quality of mystery and serenity. Was it simply that his gentle genius had spent itself in the accelerated productivity of a decade or so? Or had his new milieu with its social obligations and different artistic demands impaired his creative spirit, forever dependent on familiar faces and familiar surroundings?

Although Vuillard's oeuvre of his last thirty years appears reduced in quantity and quality, it includes a number of paintings that equal his early achievements. Almost all of these represent the artist's mother. Characteristic of such works is *The Bedroom* in which Vuillard has recaptured the poetry of conception and execution that distinguishes his paintings of the 1890's. The light in these later paintings may differ from the chiaroscuro of such interiors as the *Mother and Sister of the Artist,* the treatment of the foreground, the ceiling or other features of the picture space may have changed, but the refinement of perception, the fusion of figure and environment, the subtle interrelations between the various shapes and colors recall the masterful creations of Vuillard's youth.

G. R.

167

SELECTED BIBLIOGRAPHY

The starred entries indicate those publications referred to in abbreviated form in the text.

INTRODUCTION

*Baltimore Museum of Art, *Man and His Years,* exhibition catalogue, 1954.

*Brinckmann, A. E., *Spätwerke Grosser Meister,* Frankfurt, 1925.

*Friedlaender, Walter, *David to Delacroix* (translated by Robert Goldwater), Cambridge, Mass., 1952.

*Gantner, Joseph, "Der Alte Künstler," *Festschrift für Herbert von Einem* . . . , Berlin, 1965. (This essay was brought to our attention by Professor E. Haverkamp-Begemann, Princeton University.)

*"Youthful Works by Great Artists: A Symposium; an Exhibition . . . Honoring Professor Wolfgang Stechow," Allen Memorial Art Museum, Oberlin College, *Bulletin,* XX, No. 3, Spring 1963.

BECKMANN

Buchheim, Lothar Günther, *Max Beckmann,* Feldafing, Germany, 1959.

Lackner, Stephan, *Max Beckmann, 1884-1950,* Berlin, 1962.

St. Louis. City Art Museum, *Max Beckmann, 1948,* exhibition catalogue, 1948.

Selz, Peter, *Max Beckmann,* exhibition catalogue, Museum of Modern Art, et al, New York, 1964.

BELLOWS

Boswell, Peyton, Jr., *George Bellows,* New York, 1942.

Chicago. Art Institute, *George Bellows: Paintings, Drawings, and Prints,* exhibition catalogue, 1946.

Morgan, Charles H., *George Bellows, Painter of America,* New York, 1965.

Washington, D.C. National Gallery of Art, *George Bellows: A Retrospective Exhibition,* 1957.

BONNARD

Dauberville, Jean and Henry, *Bonnard, catalogue raisonné de l'oeuvre peint,* Paris, 1965-68.

Johnson, Lincoln F., "Pierre Bonnard and Impressionism," Baltimore Museum of Art *News,* XVII, Dec. 1953, pp. 1-6.

New York. Museum of Modern Art, *Bonnard and His Environment,* exhibition catalogue, 1964.

Rewald, John, *Pierre Bonnard,* exhibition catalogue, Museum of Modern Art, New York, and Cleveland Museum of Art, 1948.

Vaillant, Annette, *Bonnard,* (translated by Hans R. Hahnloser), Greenwich, Conn., 1966.

BRAQUE

Gieure, Maurice, *G. Braque,* Paris, 1956.

Hope, Henry R., *Georges Braque,* exhibition catalogue, Museum of Modern Art, New York, and Cleveland Museum of Art, 1949.

Richardson, John (ed.), *Georges Braque, 1882-1963, an American Tribute,* exhibition catalogue, (for the Public Education Association), New York, 1964.

CANALETTO

Constable, William G., *Canaletto: Giovanni Antonio Canal, 1697-1768,* Oxford, 1962.

Moschini, Vittorio, *Canaletto,* Milan, 1954.

Pallucchini, Rodolfo, *La Pittura Veneziana del Settecento,*.Venice and Rome, 1960.

CASSATT

Breeskin, Adelyn D., *The Graphic Work of Mary Cassatt; a Catalogue Raisonné,* New York, 1948.

Sweet, Frederick A., *Miss Mary Cassatt, Impressionist from Pennsylvania,* Norman, Okla., 1966.

Sweet, Frederick A., *Sargent, Whistler, and Mary Cassatt,* exhibition catalogue, Art Institute of Chicago, 1954.

CEZANNE

Badt, Kurt, *Die Kunst Cézannes*, Munich, 1956.

Dorival, Bernard, *Cézanne*, (translated by H. H. Thackthwaite), New York, 1948.

Fry, Roger, *Cézanne, a Study of His Development*, New York, 1927.

Schapiro, Meyer, *Paul Cézanne*, New York, 1952.

Venturi, Lionello, *Cézanne, son art — son oeuvre*, Paris, 1936.

CHAGALL

*Lake, Carlton, "Color as Love: A Portrait of Chagall," *Atlantic Monthly*, June 1958, pp. 70-74.

*Liberman, Alexander, "Chagall," *Vogue*, April 1, 1955, pp. 116-121 and 169.

Meyer, Franz, *Marc Chagall*, New York, 1963.

Sweeney, James Johnson, *Marc Chagall*, exhibition catalogue, Museum of Modern Art, New York, 1946.

Venturi, Lionello, *Marc Chagall*, New York, 1945.

CLAUDE LORRAIN

Friedlaender, Walter, *Claude Lorrain*, Berlin, 1921.

Rothlisberger, Marcel, *Claude Lorrain: The Paintings*, New Haven, Conn., 1961.

White, John, "The Landscapes of Claude," *Burlington Magazine*, XCII, February 1950, pp. 42-47.

COLE

*Cole, Thomas, "Sicilian Scenery and Antiquities," *The Knickerbocker*, 23, March 1844, pp. 103-113 and 236-244.

Flexner, James T., *That Wilder Image*, Boston, 1962.

Hartford. Wadsworth Atheneum, *Thomas Cole, One Hundred Years Later*, exhibition catalogue, 1948-49.

Noble, Louis Legrand, *The Life and Works of Thomas Cole*, (ed. Elliot S. Vessell), Cambridge, Mass., 1964.

CONSTABLE

*Reynolds, Graham, *Catalogue of the Constable Collection*, Victoria and Albert Museum, London, 1960.

Reynolds, Graham, *Constable, the Natural Painter*, New York, 1965.

COPLEY

Prown, Jules David, *John Singleton Copley*, Cambridge, Mass., 1966.

Washington, D.C. National Gallery of Art, et al, *John Singleton Copley, 1735-1815*, exhibition catalogue, 1965.

CORINTH

Berend-Corinth, Charlotte, *Die Gemälde von Lovis Corinth*, Munich, 1958.

Karlsruhe. Badischer Kunstverein, *Lovis Corinth: Das Portrait*, exhibition catalogue, 1967.

Kramer, Hilton (introd.), *Lovis Corinth*, exhibition catalogue, Gallery of Modern Art, New York, 1964.

COROT

*Barr, Alfred H., Jr., *Corot—Daumier*, exhibition catalogue, Museum of Modern Art, New York, 1930.

Bazin, Germain, *Corot*, rev. ed., Paris, 1951.

Moreau-Nélaton, Etienne, *Corot raconté par lui-même*, Paris, 1924.

Robaut, A., and Moreau-Nélaton, E., *L'Oeuvre de Corot*, Paris, 1905.

Schoeller, A., and Diéterle, J., *Corot, supplément à "L'Oeuvre de Corot" par A. Robaut et E. Moreau-Nélaton*, Paris, 1948 and 1958.

DEGAS

Boggs, Jean Sutherland, *Portraits by Degas,* Berkeley, Calif., 1962.

Lemoisne, Paul André, *Degas et son oeuvre,* Paris, 1946-49.

Rich, Daniel Catton, *Degas,* New York, 1951.

Rouart, Denis, *Degas à la recherche de sa technique,* Paris, 1945.

DELACROIX

Baudelaire, Charles, *Eugène Delacroix, His Life and Work,* (translated by J. Bernstein), New York, 1947.

Delacroix, Eugène, *Journal,* (ed. André Joubin), Paris, 1950.

Escholier, Raymond, *Delacroix; peintre, graveur, écrivain,* Paris, 1926-29.

Huyghe, René, *Delacroix,* (translated by J. Griffin), New York, 1963.

Robaut, A., and Chesneau, E., *L'Oeuvre complet d'Eugène Delacroix,* Paris, 1885.

Sérullaz, Maurice, *Mémorial de l'Exposition Eugène Delacroix . . . à l'occasion du centenaire de la mort de l'artiste,* exhibition catalogue, Louvre, Paris, 1963.

DUBUFFET

Fitzsimmons, James, "Jean Dubuffet, a Short Introduction to His Work," *Quadrum,* 4, 1957, pp. 27-50.

Paris. Musée des Arts Decoratifs, *La Donation Dubuffet,* exhibition catalogue, 1967.

*Selz, Peter, *The Work of Jean Dubuffet,* Museum of Modern Art, New York, 1962.

VAN DYCK

Cust, Lionel, *Anthony van Dyck,* London, 1900.

Gerson, H., and Ter Kuile, E. H., *Art and Architecture in Belgium, 1600-1800,* (Pelican History of Art), Baltimore, 1960.

Glück, Gustav, *Van Dyck, Des Meisters Gemälde,* (Klassiker der Kunst), Stuttgart and New York, 1931.

*Nicolson, Benedict, "Current and Forthcoming Exhibitions," *Burlington Magazine,* CIV, July 1962, pp. 310-317.

*Stechow, Wolfgang, "Two Seventeenth Century Flemish Masterpieces," *Art Quarterly,* VII, Autumn 1944, pp. 297-299.

EAKINS

Goodrich, Lloyd, *Thomas Eakins, His Life and Work,* New York, 1933.

Porter, Fairfield, *Thomas Eakins,* New York, 1959.

Washington, D.C. National Gallery of Art, et al, *Thomas Eakins, A Retrospective Exhibition,* 1961.

FRAGONARD

*Goncourt, E. and J. de, *L'Art du xviiie siècle,* Paris, 1914.

London. Royal Academy of Arts, *France in the Eighteenth Century,* exhibition catalogue, 1968.

Réau, Louis, *Fragonard, sa vie et son oeuvre,* Brussels, 1956.

Wildenstein, Georges, *The Paintings of Fragonard,* (translated by C. W. Chilton and A. L. Kitson), London, 1960.

GAINSBOROUGH

Waterhouse, Ellis, *Gainsborough,* London, 1958.

Waterhouse, Ellis, *Painting in Britain, 1530-1790,* (Pelican History of Art), Baltimore, 1953.

GAUGUIN

Goldwater, Robert, *Paul Gauguin,* New York, 1957.

Rewald, John, *Gauguin,* New York, 1938.

Wildenstein, Georges, *Gauguin,* Paris, 1964.

VAN GOGH

*Van Gogh, Vincent, *The Complete Letters of Vincent Van Gogh,* (translated by C. de Dood), Greenwich, Conn., 1958.

La Faille, J. B. de, *Vincent Van Gogh,* (Hyperion), Paris and New York, 1939.

Rewald, John, *Post-Impressionism from Van Gogh to Gauguin,* 2nd ed., New York, 1962.

*Schapiro, Meyer, *Vincent Van Gogh,* New York, 1950.

GORKY

*Hartley, Anthony (ed. and trans.), *The Penguin Book of French Verse,* III, Middlesex, England, 1958.

Levy, Julien, *Arshile Gorky,* New York, 1968.

Rosenberg, Harold, *Arshile Gorky, the Man, the Time, the Idea,* New York, 1962.

Rubin, William, "Arshile Gorky, Surrealism and the New American Painting," *Art International,* VII, Feb. 25, 1963, pp. 27-38.

Schwabacher, Ethel K., *Arshile Gorky,* New York, 1957.

*Seitz, William C., *Arshile Gorky, Paintings, Drawings, Studies,* exhibition catalogue, Museum of Modern Art, New York, and Washington Gallery of Modern Art, 1962.

GOYA

Beruete y Moret, A. de, *Goya,* (translated by S. Brinton), Boston and London, 1922.

*Gudiol, José, *Goya,* (translated by Priscilla Muller), New York, 1964.

Malraux, André, *Saturn: An Essay on Goya,* (translated by C. W. Chilton), London, 1957.

Mayer, A. L., *Francisco de Goya,* London and Toronto, 1924.

EL GRECO

Bronstein, Leo, *El Greco,* New York, 1950.

Legendre, M., and Hartmann, A., *Domenikos Theotokopoulos Called El Greco,* (ed. André Gloeckner), Paris, 1937.

Wethey, Harold E., *El Greco and His School,* Princeton, N.J., 1962.

GREUZE

*Goncourt, E. and J. de, *L'Art du xviiie siècle,* Paris, 1914.

Hoffman, Grace, "The Painter Greuze and His Portrait of the Marquise de Besons," Baltimore Museum of Art *News,* XII, April 1949, pp. 1-3.

Mauclair, Camille, *Jean-Baptiste Greuze,* (with catalogue by Jean Martin), Paris, 1905.

Munhall, Edgar, "Greuze's Portrait of Comtesse Mollien, Study of a Motif," Baltimore Museum of Art *News,* XXVI, Fall 1962, pp. 14-23.

GRIS

Kahnweiler, Daniel-Henry, *Juan Gris, His Life and Work,* (translated by Douglas Cooper), New York, 1947.

Soby, James Thrall, *Juan Gris,* exhibition catalogue, Museum of Modern Art, et al, New York, 1958.

GUARDI

Constable, William G., "Two Paintings by Marieschi," Baltimore Museum of Art *News*, XI, Jan. 1948, pp. 1-4.

*Levey, Michael, *Painting in Eighteenth Century Venice*, London, 1959.

Mahon, Denis, "When did Francesco Guardi Become a 'Vedutista'?" *Burlington Magazine*, CX, Feb. 1968, pp. 69-73.

Moschini, Vittorio, *Francesco Guardi*, Milan, 1952.

*Pallucchini, Rodolfo, "A Proposito della Mostra Bergamasca del Marieschi," *Arte Veneta*, XX, 1966, pp. 314-325.

Pallucchini, Rodolfo, *La Pittura Veneziana del Settecento*, Venice and Rome, 1960.

Pignatti, Terisio, "The Contemporaneity of the Eighteenth-Century Venetian 'Vedutisti'," *Art International*, XI, Christmas 1967, pp. 24-25.

Pilo, Giuseppe Maria, "La Mostra dei Vedutisti Veneziani del Settecento," *Arte Veneta*, XXI, 1967, pp. 269-277.

*Zampetti, Pietro, *I Vedutisti Veneziani del Settecento*, exhibition catalogue, Palazzo Ducale. Venice, 1967.

HALS

Slive, Seymour, *Frans Hals, Exhibition on the Occasion of the Centenary of the Municipal Museum at Haarlem*, Frans Halsmuseum, Haarlem, 1962.

*Thiel, P. J. J. van, "Frans Hals' Portret van de Leidse Rederijkersnar, Pieter Cornelisz. van der Morsch, alias Piero (1543-1629). Een bijdrage tot de Ikonologie van de bokking," *Oud-Holland*, LXXVI, 1961.

Valentiner, Wilhelm R., *Frans Hals*, (Klassiker der Kunst), 2nd ed., Berlin and Leipzig, 1923.

Valentiner, Wilhelm R., *Frans Hals Paintings in America*, Westport, Conn., 1936.

HOFMANN

Ashton, Dore, " 'Summer Night's Bliss,' a New Painting by Hans Hofmann," Baltimore Museum of Art *News*, XXV, Spring 1962, pp. 4-8.

Hunter, Sam (ed.), *Hans Hofmann*, (with five essays by the artist), New York, 1963.

Rosenberg, Harold, *The Anxious Object, Art Today and Its Audience*, New York, 1964.

Seitz, William C., *Hans Hofmann*, (with selected writings by the artist), New York, 1963.

HOMER

Boston. Museum of Fine Arts, et al, *A Retrospective Exhibition, Winslow Homer*, 1959.

Gardner, Albert Ten Eyck, *Winslow Homer, American Artist, His World and His Work*, New York, 1961.

Goodrich, Lloyd, *Winslow Homer*, New York, 1959.

HOPPER

Barr, Alfred H., Jr. (introd.), *Edward Hopper, Retrospective Exhibition*, Museum of Modern Art, New York, 1933.

Goodrich, Lloyd, *Edward Hopper*, exhibition catalogue, Whitney Museum of American Art, New York, 1964.

O'Doherty, Brian, "Portrait: Edward Hopper," *Art In America*, 52, Dec. 1964, pp. 68-88.

INGRES

*Delécluze, M. E. J., *Louis David, son école et son temps*, Paris, 1855.

King, Edward S., "Ingres as Classicist," *The Journal of the Walters Art Gallery*, V, 1942, pp. 68-113.

Lapauze, Henry, *Ingres, sa vie et son oeuvre, (1780-1867), d'après des documents inédits*, Paris, 1911.

*Lapauze, Henry, *Le Roman d'amour de M. Ingres*, Paris, 1910.

*Mongan, Agnes, *Ingres, Centennial Exhibition, 1867-1967*, Fogg Art Museum, Cambridge, Mass., 1967.

Paris. Petit Palais, *Ingres*, exhibition catalogue, 1968.

Wildenstein, Georges, *Ingres*, London, 1954.

INNESS

*Cikovsky, Nicolai, Jr. (introd.), *The Paintings of George Inness 1844-94*, exhibition catalogue, University Art Museum, Austin, Tex., 1966.

Ireland, LeRoy, *The Works of George Inness; An Illustrated Catalogue Raisonné*, Austin, Tex., 1965.

*"Mr. Inness on Art-Matters," *Art Journal*, V, 1879, pp. 374-377.

*"A Painter on Painting," [An Interview with George Inness], *Harper's New Monthly Magazine*, LVI, 1878, pp. 458-461.

KANDINSKY

Grohmann, Will, *Wassily Kandinsky: Life and Work*, (translated by N. Guterman), New York, 1958.

Kandinsky, Vasily, *On the Spiritual in Art*, New York, 1946.

New York. Solomon R. Guggenheim Museum, *Vasily Kandinsky 1866-1944, A Retrospective Exhibition*, 1962.

KIRCHNER

Gordon, Donald E., *Ernst Ludwig Kirchner*, Cambridge, Mass., (publ. date, Dec. 1968).

Gordon, Donald E., "Kirchner in Dresden," *Art Bulletin*, XLVIII, Sept.-Dec. 1966, pp. 335-366.

Grohmann, Will, *E. L. Kirchner*, (translated by I. Falk), New York, 1961.

Myers, Bernard S., *The German Expressionists*, New York, 1957.

Valentiner, Wilhelm R., *E. L. Kirchner, German Expressionist*, exhibition catalogue, North Carolina Museum of Art, Raleigh, 1958.

KLEE

*Grohmann, Will, *Paul Klee*, New York, n.d.

Haftmann, Werner, *The Mind and Work of Paul Klee*, London, 1954.

Spiller, Jürg (ed.), *Paul Klee: The Thinking Eye*, New York and London, 1961.

KLINE

Ashton, Dore, "Franz Kline," *Cimaise*, No. 53, May-June 1961, pp. 70-83.

*De Kooning, Elaine (introd.), *Franz Kline Memorial Exhibition*, Washington Gallery of Modern Art, et al, 1962.

Goodnough, Robert, "Kline Paints a Picture," *Art News*, 51, Dec. 1952, pp. 36-39 and 63-64.

Oeri, Georgine, "Notes on Franz Kline," *Quadrum*, 12, 1961, pp. 93-102.

LEGER

Cooper, Douglas, *Fernand Léger et le nouvel espace*, London, 1949.

Descargues, Pierre, *Fernand Léger*, Paris, 1955.

Kuh, Katherine, *Léger*, Urbana, Ill., 1953.

New York. Solomon R. Guggenheim Museum, *Fernand Léger: Five Themes and Variations*, exhibition catalogue, 1962.

MAGNASCO

Geiger, Benno, *Magnasco*, Bergamo, 1949.

Sitwell, Osbert, "The Magnasco Society," *Apollo*, LXXIX, May 1964, pp. 378-390.

MANET

Hamilton, George Heard, *Manet and His Critics*, New Haven, Conn., 1954.

Hanson, Anne Coffin, *Edouard Manet, 1832-1883*, exhibition catalogue, Philadelphia Museum of Art and Art Institute of Chicago, 1966.

Jamot, P., and Wildenstein, G., *Manet*, Paris, 1932.

Moreau-Nélaton, Etienne, *Manet raconté par lui-même*, Paris, 1926.

MARIN

Boston. Institute of Contemporary Art, *John Marin, a Retrospective Exhibition*, 1947.

Helm, MacKinley, *John Marin*, Boston, 1948.

MATISSE

Barr, Alfred H., Jr., *Matisse, His Art and His Public,* New York, 1951.

Diehl, Gaston, *Henri Matisse,* Paris, 1954.

Gowing, Lawrence, *Henri Matisse: 64 Paintings,* exhibition catalogue, Museum of Modern Art, New York, 1966.

Leymarie, Jean, et al, *Henri Matisse,* exhibition catalogue, (organized by the UCLA Art Council and the UCLA Art Galleries), Berkeley and Los Angeles, 1966.

Reverdy, P., and Duthuit, G., *The Last Works of Henri Matisse,* New York, 1958.

MIRO

Dupin, Jacques, *Joan Miró,* (translated by N. Guterman), London, 1962.

Greenberg, Clement, *Joan Miró,* New York, 1948.

Soby, James Thrall, *Joan Miró,* New York, 1959.

Sweeney, James Johnson, *Joan Miró,* New York, 1941.

MONDRIAN

*Blok, Cornelis, *Mondriaan in de collectie van het Haags Gemeentemuseum — catalogus 1964,* The Hague, 1964.

Jaffé, H. L. C., *De Styl 1917-1931,* Amsterdam, 1956.

Mondrian, Piet, *Plastic Art and Pure Plastic Art (1937) and Other Essays (1941-43),* 2nd ed., New York, 1947.

*Seuphor, Michel, *Piet Mondrian: Life and Work,* New York, 1956.

Welsh, Robert P., *Piet Mondrian (1872-1944),* exhibition catalogue, Art Gallery of Toronto, 1966.

MONET

Geffroy, G., *Claude Monet, sa vie, son temps, son oeuvre,* Paris, 1924.

*Rewald, John, *The History of Impressionism,* rev. ed., New York, 1961.

*Seitz, William C., *Claude Monet,* New York, 1960.

Venturi, Lionello, *Les Archives de l'impressionnisme,* Paris and New York, 1939.

PEALE

Elam, Charles H., *The Peale Family: Three Generations of American Artists,* exhibition catalogue, Detroit Institute of Arts, 1967.

Sellers, Charles Coleman, *Charles Willson Peale,* Philadelphia, 1947.

*Sellers, Charles Coleman, *Portraits and Miniatures by Charles Willson Peale,* Philadelphia, 1952.

PIAZZETTA

Pallucchini, Rodolfo, *Piazzetta,* Milan, 1956.

Wittkower, Rudolf, *Art and Architecture in Italy, 1600 to 1750,* (Pelican History of Art), Baltimore, 1958.

PICASSO

Barr, Alfred H., Jr., *Picasso, Fifty Years of His Art,* New York, 1946.

Boggs, Jean Sutherland, *Picasso and Man,* exhibition catalogue, Art Gallery of Toronto, 1964.

Daix, P., and Boudaille, G., *Picasso, the Blue and Rose Periods, A Catalogue Raisonné of the Paintings, 1900-1906,* (translated by P. Pool), rev. ed., Greenwich, Conn., 1967.

Duncan, David Douglas, *Picasso's Picassos,* New York, 1961.

Paris. Grand Palais and Petit Palais, *Hommage à Pablo Picasso,* exhibition catalogue, 3rd ed., 1966.

Penrose, Roland, *Picasso: His Life and Work,* New York, 1959.

Zervos, Christian, *Pablo Picasso,* Vols. 1-18, Paris, 1932-67.

PISSARRO

Pissarro, L., and Venturi, L., *Camille Pissarro; son art — son oeuvre*, Paris, 1939.

Rewald, John, *Camille Pissarro*, New York, 1963.

Rosenthal, Gertrude, "The Path by the River," Baltimore Museum of Art *News*, VIII, Jan. 1946, pp. 4-6.

POLLOCK

O'Connor, Francis V., *Jackson Pollock*, exhibition catalogue, Museum of Modern Art, New York, 1967.

O'Connor, Francis V., "The Genesis of Jackson Pollock: 1912-1943," *Artforum*, V, No. 9, May 1967, pp. 16-23.

O'Hara, Frank, *Jackson Pollock*, New York, 1959.

Robertson, Bryan, *Jackson Pollock*, New York, 1960.

Rubin, William, "Jackson Pollock and the Modern Tradition," (4 parts), *Artforum*, V, Nos. 6-9, Feb.-May 1967.

POUSSIN

*Blunt, Anthony, *Art and Architecture in France, 1500-1700*, London, 1953.

Blunt, Anthony, *Exposition Nicolas Poussin*, exhibition catalogue, 2nd rev. ed., Louvre, Paris, 1960.

*Blunt, Anthony, *Nicolas Poussin*, (The A. W. Mellon Lectures in the Fine Arts), New York, 1967.

Blunt, Anthony, *The Paintings of Nicolas Poussin*, London, 1966.

Chastel, André (ed.), *Nicholas Poussin*, (Centre National de la Recherche Scientifique Colloques Internationaux), Paris, 1958.

Friedlaender, Walter F., *Nicholas Poussin; a New Approach*, New York, 1966.

*Josephus, Flavius, *Jewish Antiquities*, (The Loeb Classical Library edition), London, 1930.

Mahon, Denis, "Poussiniana. Afterthoughts Arising from the Exhibition," *Gazette des Beaux-Arts*, LX, July 1962, pp. 1-138.

Milliken, William M., "Moses Sweetening the Waters of Marah," Baltimore Museum of Art *News*, XXII, Oct. 1958, pp. 3-11.

REMBRANDT

Bauch, Kurt, *Rembrandt, Gemälde*, Berlin, 1966.

*Benesch, Otto, *The Drawings of Rembrandt*, London, 1954.

Benesch, Otto, "Worldly and Religious Portraits in Rembrandt's Late Art," *Art Quarterly*, XIX, Winter 1956, pp. 334-355.

Bredius, Abraham, *The Paintings of Rembrandt*, New York, 1942.

Clark, Kenneth, *Rembrandt and the Italian Renaissance*, (The Wrightsman Lectures), New York, 1966.

Rosenberg, Jakob, *Rembrandt, Life and Work*, rev. ed., London, 1964.

Slive, Seymour, *Rembrandt and His Critics: 1630-1730*, The Hague, 1953.

Valentiner, Wilhelm R., *Rembrandt Paintings in America*, New York, 1932.

RENOIR

Drucker, Michel, *Renoir*, Paris, 1955.

Meier-Graefe, Julius, *Renoir*, Leipzig, 1929.

*Pach, Walter (introd.), *Pierre Auguste Renoir*, New York, 1950.

*Rewald, John, *The History of Impressionism*, rev. ed., New York, 1961.

Vollard, Ambroise, *La Vie et l'oeuvre de Pierre-Auguste Renoir*, Paris, 1919.

REYNOLDS

Hudson, Derek, *Sir Joshua Reynolds, a Personal Study*, London, 1958.

Waterhouse, Ellis, *Painting in Britain, 1530-1790*, (Pelican History of Art), Baltimore, 1953.

Waterhouse, Ellis, *Reynolds*, London, 1941.

RUBENS

Belgian Center for Sixteenth- and Seventeenth-Century Fine Arts (ed.), *Corpus Rubenianum Ludwig Burchard: An Illustrated Catalogue Raisonné of the Work of Peter Paul Rubens,* (26 volumes in preparation), 1968-

Brussels. Musées Royaux des Beaux-Arts de Belgique, *Le Siècle de Rubens,* exhibition catalogue, 1965.

Burckhardt, Jakob, *Recollections of Rubens,* (Phaidon), New York, 1950.

Evers, H. G., *Rubens und seine Werke, Neue Forschungen,* Brussels, 1943.

Goris, J., and Held, J. S., *Rubens in America,* New York, 1947.

*Held, Julius S., "Rubens' 'King of Tunis' and Vermeyen's Portrait of Mulay Ahmad," *Art Quarterly,* III, Spring 1940, pp. 173-181.

Rooses, M., *L'Oeuvre de P. P. Rubens,* Antwerp, 1886-92.

RUISDAEL

*Hind, Arthur M., *Rembrandt's Etchings: An Essay and a Catalogue,* London, 1912.

Rosenberg, Jakob, et al, *Dutch Art and Architecture, 1600-1800,* (Pelican History of Art), Baltimore, 1966.

Rosenberg, Jakob, *Jacob van Ruisdael,* Berlin, 1928.

Stechow, Wolfgang, *Dutch Landscape Painting of the Seventeenth Century,* London, 1966.

SARGENT

Mount, Charles Merrill, *John Singer Sargent, a Biography,* New York, 1955.

Sweet, Frederick A., *Sargent, Whistler, and Mary Cassatt,* exhibition catalogue, Art Institute of Chicago, 1954.

Washington, D.C. Corcoran Gallery of Art, *The Private World of John Singer Sargent,* exhibition catalogue, 1964.

STROZZI

Milkovich, Michael, *Bernardo Strozzi, Paintings and Drawings, Dedication Exhibition of the University Art Gallery,* Binghamton, N.Y., 1967.

Mortari, Luisa, *Bernardo Strozzi,* Rome, 1966.

STUART

Mason, George C., *The Life and Works of Gilbert Stuart,* New York, 1894.

Mount, Charles Merrill, *Gilbert Stuart, a Biography,* New York. 1964.

Park, Lawrence, *Gilbert Stuart, an Illustrated Description List of His Work,* New York, 1926.

Washington, D.C. National Gallery of Art and Rhode Island School of Design, *Gilbert Stuart, Portraitist of the Young Republic, 1755-1828,* exhibition catalogue, 1967.

TIEPOLO

Morassi, Antonio, *A Complete Catalogue of the Paintings of G. B. Tiepolo Including Pictures by His Pupils and Followers Wrongly Attributed to Him,* London, 1962.

Pallucchini, Rodolfo, *Pittura Veneziana del Settecento,* Venice and Rome, 1960.

TOBEY

Palo Alto. Stanford University, Department of Art and Architecture, *Mark Tobey: Paintings from the Collection of Joyce and Arthur Dahl,* exhibition catalogue, 1967.

Seitz, William C., *Mark Tobey,* New York, 1962.

Tobey, Mark, *The World of a Market,* Seattle, Wash., 1964.

TOULOUSE-LAUTREC

Huisman, P., and Dortu, M. G., *Lautrec by Lautrec,* New York, 1964.

Jourdain, F., and Adhémar, J., *T-Lautrec,* Paris, 1952.

Joyant, Maurice, *Henri de Toulouse-Lautrec 1864-1901,* Paris, 1926.

TURNER

Finberg, A. J., *The Life of J. M. W. Turner, R.A.,* 2nd ed., revised by Hilda Finberg, Oxford, 1961.

*Gowing, Lawrence, *Turner: Imagination and Reality,* exhibition catalogue, Museum of Modern Art, New York, 1966.

Lindsay, Jack, *J. M. W. Turner: His Life and Work,* Greenwich, Conn., 1966.

Rothenstein, J., and Butlin, M., *Turner,* New York, 1964.

VIGEE-LEBRUN

Florisoone, Michel, *Le Dix-huitième siècle: La Peinture française,* Paris, 1948.

Helm, W. H., *Vigée-Lebrun, Her Life, Works, and Friendships,* London, 1916.

*Vigée-Lebrun, Elisabeth, *Souvenirs,* Paris, 1869.

VILLON

Lassaigne, Jacques, *Jacques Villon,* Paris, 1950.

Lieberman, William S., *Jacques Villon: His Graphic Art,* exhibition catalogue, Museum of Modern Art, New York, 1953.

Vallier, Dora, *Jacques Villon, oeuvres de 1897 à 1956,* Paris, 1957.

VUILLARD

Chastel, André, "Interior: The Bedroom by Vuillard," Baltimore Museum of Art *News,* XIV, Dec. 1950, pp. 1-3.

Chastel, André, *Vuillard, 1868-1940,* Paris, 1946.

Munich. Haus der Kunst, *Edouard Vuillard, Xavier Roussel,* exhibition catalogue, 1968.

Ritchie, Andrew C., *Edouard Vuillard,* exhibition catalogue, Museum of Modern Art, New York, and Cleveland Museum of Art, 1954.

*Roger-Marx, Claude, *Vuillard: His Life and Work,* New York, 1946.

WEST

*Chamberlin, Arthur B., *George Romney,* New York, 1910.

Evans, Grose, *Benjamin West and the Taste of His Times,* Carbondale, Ill., 1959.

Flexner, James T., "Benjamin West's American Neo-Classicism," *New York Historical Society Quarterly,* XXXVI, 1952, pp. 5-41.

*Kimball, Fiske, "Benjamin West au Salon de 1802," *Gazette des Beaux-Arts,* VII, June 1932, pp. 403-410.

WHISTLER

Eddy, Arthur J., *Recollections and Impressions of James A. McNeill Whistler,* Philadelphia and London, 1903.

Sutton, Denys, *James McNeill Whistler, Paintings, Etchings, Pastels and Watercolours,* London, 1966.

Sweet, Frederick A., *James McNeill Whistler,* exhibition catalogue, Art Institute of Chicago, 1968.

Whistler, James A. McNeill, *The Gentle Art of Making Enemies,* London, 1890.

INDEX OF ARTISTS

CATALOGUE NUMBERS	NAME	PAGES
91-92	Beckmann	114-115
93-94	Bellows	116-117
95-96	Bonnard	118-119
97-98	Braque	120-121
19-20	Canaletto	38-39
49-50	Cassatt	70-71
51-52	Cézanne	72-73
99-100	Chagall	122-123
3-4	Claude Lorrain	20-21
53-54	Cole	74-75
55-56	Constable	76-77
21-22	Copley	40-41
101-102	Corinth	124-125
57-58	Corot	78-79
59-60	Degas	80-81
61-62	Delacroix	82-83
103-104	Dubuffet	126-127
5-6	Van Dyck	22-23
63-64	Eakins	84-85
23-24	Fragonard	42-43
25-26	Gainsborough	44-45
65-66	Gauguin	86-87
67-68	Van Gogh	88-89
105-106	Gorky	128-129
27-28	Goya	46-47
1-2	El Greco	16-17
29-30	Greuze	48-49
107-108	Gris	130-131
31-32	Guardi, Francesco	50-51
7-8	Hals	24-25
109-110	Hofmann	132-133
69-70	Homer	90-91
111-112	Hopper	134-135
71-72	Ingres	92-93
73-74	Inness	94-95
113-114	Kandinsky	136-137
115-116	Kirchner	138-139
117-118	Klee	140-141

119-120	Kline	142-143
	✓ Lautrec (see Toulouse-Lautrec)	
121-122	Léger	144-145
	Lorrain, Claude (see Claude)	
33-34	Magnasco	52-53
75-76	✓ Manet	96-97
123-124	Marin	146-147
125-127	✓ Matisse	148-151
128-129	Miró	152-153
130-131	Mondrian	154-155
77-78	✓ Monet	98-99
35-36	Peale, Charles Willson	54-55
37-38	Piazzetta	56-57
132-135	✓ Picasso	156-159
79-80	Pissarro	100-101
136-137	Pollock	160-161
9-10	Poussin	26-27
11-12	Rembrandt	28-29
81-82	Renoir	102-103
39-40	Reynolds	58-59
13-14	Rubens	30-31
15-16	Ruisdael	32-33
83-84	Sargent	104-105
17-18	Strozzi	34-35
41-42	Stuart	60-61
43-44	Tiepolo, Giovanni Battista	62-63
138-139	Tobey	162-163
85-86	✓ Toulouse-Lautrec	106-107
87-88	Turner	108-109
45-46	Vigée-Lebrun	64-65
140-141	Villon	164-165
142-143	Vuillard	166-167
47-48	West	66-67
89-90	Whistler	110-111

DESIGN
Omni Associates

LITHOGRAPHY
Vintone-Gravure Process
Vinmar Lithographing Company

TYPOGRAPHY
Optima and Optima Semi-Bold
Service Composition Company

BINDING
Graphic Arts Finishing Company
and Moore and Company, Inc.

PAPERS
Text Pages — Warren's Lustro Dull Enamel
End Papers for Case Bound Edition —
Strathmore's Grandee
Cover for Case Bound Edition —
Arrestox Black Buckram
Cover for Paper Bound Edition —
Strathmore's Grandee Duplex